# A HOLY

## HOLINESS:
### Calling People to a Life of Significance

# PASSION

Compiled by

# NEIL B. WISEMAN

and

# CHARLES E. ZINK

Beacon Hill Press of Kansas City
Kansas City, Missouri

Copyright 2004
Beacon Hill Press of Kansas City
Kansas City, Missouri

ISBN 083-412-1409

Printed in the United States of America

Cover Design: Ted Ferguson

## Bible Credits

Unless otherwise indicated, all Scripture references are from the King James Version (KJV).

Permission to quote from the following additional copyrighted versions of the Bible is acknowledged with appreciation:

The Bible: A New Translation (MOFFATT). Copyright 1922, 1924, 1925, 1935 by Harper and Row, Publishers, Incorporated. Copyright 1950, 1952, 1953, 1954 by James A. R. Moffatt.

The New American Standard Bible® (NASB®), © copyright The Lockman Foundation 1960, 1962, 1963, 1968, 1971, 1972, 1973, 1975, 1977, 1995.

The Holy Bible, New International Version® (NIV®). Copyright © 1973, 1978, 1984 by International Bible Society. Used by permission of Zondervan Publishing House. All rights reserved.

The New King James Version (NKJV). Copyright © 1979, 1980, 1982 Thomas Nelson, Inc.

The New Revised Standard Version (NRSV) of the Bible, copyright 1989 by the Division of Christian Education of the National Council of the Churches of Christ in the USA. Used by permission. All rights reserved.

The New Testament in Modern English (PHILLIPS), Revised Student Edition, by J. B. Phillips, translator. Copyright 1958, 1960, 1972 by J. B. Phillips.

The Revised Standard Version (RSV) of the Bible, copyright 1946, 1952, 1971 by the Division of the National Council of the Churches of Christ in the USA.

The Message (TM). Copyright © 1993. Used by permission of NavPress Publishing Group.

The New Testament in Modern Speech (WEYMOUTH). Copyright 1929 by Harper and Brothers, New York.

### Library of Congress Cataloging-in-Publication Data

A holy passion : holiness : calling people to a life of significance : a palcon resource book for Nazarene ministers / compiled by Neil B. Wiseman and Charles E. Zink.
   p. cm.
 "A Palcon resource book for Nazarene ministers."
 ISBN 0-8341-2140-9 (pbk.)
 1. Holiness. I. Wiseman, Neil B. II. Zink, Charles E.

BT767.H65 2004
234'.8—dc22

2004003074

10  9  8  7  6  5  4  3  2  1

# CONTENTS

# FOREWORD

## Challenge of Our Mission

Dear Sisters and Brothers,

Please allow me to express my gratitude for your faithfulness to this important calling of shepherding believers in the Church of the Nazarene. Your ministry is vital to the redemptive work of the Kingdom, both in your local community and in our particular branch of Christ's Body. Without you and your partners in ministry, both clergy and laity, all efforts to maintain our heritage, to uphold our core values, and to carry out our mission would be in vain. I am optimistic about the future of the Church of the Nazarene, primarily because of the quality of my colleagues in ministry. God has blessed and gifted His Church by calling you to lead her.

As you peruse these three volumes prepared for PALCON 2004, I hope you will conclude as I have, that the subjects they address are vital to our ministry in the Church of the Nazarene. The degree of your faithfulness and mine to our preaching task, to our role as shepherds, and to our doctrine of holiness, will have a direct effect on the extent to which current and future generations will identify and distinguish themselves as a Missional, Christian, Holiness people.

Let us covenant together that the labors of these authors, whose ministries were and are so Spirit-filled, will not fall to the ground. Let us pray for guidance and inspiration from the Holy Spirit as we read their words, absorb their passion, and proceed as the inheritors of their spiritual legacy. May you find yourself refreshed, stimulated, and moved to action by what you read in these pages.

In His Peace,
Charles E. Zink
Director, Clergy Development

# PREFACE

## HOLINESS: ISN'T QUALITY OF LIFE THE ISSUE?

THIS BOOK IS INTENDED to be a resource, a primer, an anthology of writings concerning the life of holy wholeness. It deals with holiness as the Father's glad provision of cleansing and power that provides for believers a quality life and a victorious translation into eternity.

While we study holiness as a doctrine, there would be no need of doctrine if there were not a holiness life to be lived. Jesus described it as the life more abundant—a better life than you ever dreamed of (see John 10:10, TM). The apostle Paul called it a "wildly extravagant life—a grand setting-everything-right kind of living" (Rom. 5:7, TM).

God raised up the Church of the Nazarene to help people find their way into such a holy, pure life. That's our church's reason for being. Read Nazarene history, listen to Nazarene stories, sing Nazarene songs, research Nazarene writings, and interview Nazarene people about their parents and grandparents, and you will find the holiness doctrine and experience to be the essential essence of this denomination. Every church building, every college campus, every district camp, and every mission stands as a silent witness to the sacrifices of persons who gave themselves in happy abandonment to the cause of holiness.

Those Nazarene pioneers never intended that what they left us and our children would become a nice, generic, evangelical denomination. Rather, they intended for us to be a Holiness denomination, a family of churches that would preach and teach and live the holiness way, the way of love made perfect, the way of authentic Christlikeness, the way of purity and power, the way of death to self-sovereignty and life in Christ. A way of wholeness, joy, and meaning.

In this book, chapter by chapter you will find ideas to improve your holiness preaching. You will find helps for leading persons into the experience of holiness. Should you not have a holy heart, a settled will, and a crucified self—find your way into the experience by the grace of God. Let's protect the message and the life of holiness given by our spiritual parents.

As founding director of the first PALCON in 1976-77, it gives me indescribable satisfaction to be involved in PALCON 2004. Part of my responsibility for this great PALCON series was selecting and editing these chapters on holiness. Some of this material is relatively new, and other chapters are part of Nazarene history. (They have been edited only slightly, and therefore retain the writers' original work, in some cases complete with dated references and non-gender-inclusive language.)

My joy overflows and my heart is filled with gratitude for the accumulated impact the various PALCONs have had on our church. And I am glad to be a small part of PALCON 2004.

—Neil B. Wiseman

# 1

# DISCOVERING CHRISTIAN HOLINESS
## —Revisiting the Basics—

## Albert F. Harper

CAROLINE TESTIFIES:

It is surprising how blind a person can be even with 20/20 vision. There I stood looking directly at the envelope on my desk, but I couldn't see it. I don't know how long I hunted for it, but I know it was longer than necessary. That's the way it was with my spiritual life.

As a young adult I realized the great need of my soul for a Savior. Although my life seemed together, it was apart. I could not ignore the longing in my empty spirit. Then He came. Jesus came into my heart, and forgave my sins. I was in His presence, but I still couldn't truly see Him.

I spent years searching for God's grace that would give me full release from the sin of a double mind and a divided heart. I searched the Scriptures, and they left me craving more. I searched at revival services and in camp meetings. Even in the presence of all that glory, I still could not see.

And then, having asked the Holy Spirit to remove the blindness of my soul, light was given. I saw myself as He saw me. The sight was not pleasant. It revealed a sinful nature pulling me from the Christ I longed to serve completely. I saw the rotten attitudes that cluttered the heart I wanted to be clean. I saw the selfishness that clogged the spirit that I wanted to be free.

But as my eyes began to see these barriers clearly, I opened my heart to the Holy Spirit's work—and He gave my soul 20/20 vision. I can now see beyond myself. I see His face—and His reflection is slowly becoming mine.

Spiritual blindness almost drained my spirit of every beautiful plan God has for my life. But now I am thankful my soul can sing with multitudes who have gone before, "I once was blind, but now I see"—because of His amazing grace.

I am glad this young mother attended a church where she learned about holiness. I am glad that she read her Bible and discovered Paul's prayer:

May God himself, the God of peace, sanctify you through and through. May your whole spirit, soul, and body be kept blameless at the coming of our Lord Jesus Christ. The one who calls you is faithful and he will do it *(1 Thess. 5:23-24, NIV)*.

I rejoice that the truth of entire sanctification disturbed her until she was not content to continue in a life of division and defeat. I am glad God has given us His grace of Christian holiness.

## WHAT IS CHRISTIAN HOLINESS?

Holiness is a grace because it is one of God's gifts to us. But how are we to understand its meaning? To be holy is to be Christlike in spirit. To be holy is to be morally like the God whom we love and serve—to have His spirit and His attitudes. To be holy is to be like God—dead set against every kind of sin. To be holy is to be like God in having my intentions and attitudes motivated by His spirit of love.

To be holy is to be whole, as God intends His child to be. God's purpose for every man and woman is that our lives shall be rich and fulfilled. We find this completeness and satisfaction only as we allow Him to mold our attitudes and actions.

Because He loves us, God says, "Ye shall be holy." Because He wants to make us like himself, He says, "Ye shall be holy; for I am holy."

## WHAT THE BIBLE TEACHES ABOUT HOLINESS

### Old Testament Teaching

Because God wants to give us something of His own holy character, He tells us about it in the Scriptures. Early in the Old Testament He reveals His plan for those who are His people: "I am the LORD your God: ye shall therefore sanctify yourselves, and ye shall be holy; for I am holy" (Lev. 11:44). From this point on, the message of scriptural holiness comes through clearly.

To Israel God promised,

> Then will I sprinkle clean water upon you, and ye shall be clean: from all your filthiness . . . will I cleanse you. . . . I will put my spirit within you, and cause you to walk in my statutes, and ye shall keep my judgments, and do them *(Ezek. 36:25, 27)*.

Such a holy heart is a gift from God.

In the face of his outbroken sin, David knew that he needed help from God that went beyond forgiveness for his sinful act. He prayed: "Hide thy face from my sins, and blot out all mine iniquities. Create in me a clean heart, O God; and renew a right spirit within me" (Ps. 51:9-10).

## The New Testament Teachings of Jesus

God offers His gift of a cleansed spirit because fallen man has a deep need. Jesus knew that evil deeds arise from an evil condition in the depraved human spirit. He tells us,

> From within, out of men's hearts, come evil thoughts, sexual immorality, theft, murder, adultery, greed, malice, deceit, lewdness, envy, slander, arrogance, and folly. All these evils come from inside and make a man "unclean" *(Mark 7:21-23, NIV)*.

The Bible teaches that it is necessary to have our carnal spirits cleaned up if we are to be Christlike. Jesus tells us that this inner purity is the preparation for fellowship with the Heavenly Father: "Blessed are the pure in heart: for they shall see God" (Matt. 5:8).

The Scriptures also show us that heart-cleansing is given to us through the work of God's Holy Spirit. John the Baptist declared, "I baptize you with water for repentance. But after me will come one who is more powerful than I . . . He will baptize you with the Holy Spirit and with fire" (Matt. 3:11, NIV).

To do the whole will of God, we need to be filled with the Holy Spirit— and God yearns to meet our need. Jesus said, "If you then, though you are evil, know how to give good gifts to your children, how much more will your Father in heaven give the Holy Spirit to those who ask him!" (Luke 11:13, NIV).

To His early followers Jesus promised: "I will pray the Father, and he shall give you another Comforter, that he may abide with you for ever; even the Spirit of truth" (John 14:16-17). A little later that same evening Jesus prayed to the Father:

> I pray not that thou shouldest take them out of the world, but that thou shouldest keep them from the evil. They are not of the world, even as I am not of the world. Sanctify them through thy truth: thy word is truth *(John 17:15-17)*.

**JESUS PRAYED THAT WE MIGHT BE SANCTIFIED BY THE CLEANSING HOLY SPIRIT.**

Jesus prayed that we might be sanctified by the cleansing Holy Spirit, but He makes it clear that we must fulfill the conditions for His coming: "Behold, I send the promise of my Father upon you: but tarry ye . . . until ye be endued with power from on high" (Luke 24:49).

Describing these instructions in another place, Luke writes of Jesus' directive,

> Do not leave Jerusalem, but wait for the gift my Father promised, which you have heard me speak about. For John baptized with water, but in a few days you will be baptized with the Holy Spirit *(Acts 1:4-5, NIV)*.

At this time Jesus also explained why it was so important to Him that His followers tarry until they were baptized with the Holy Spirit: "You will receive power when the Holy Spirit comes on you; and you will be my witnesses in Jerusalem, and in all Judea and Samaria, and to the ends of the earth" (v. 8, NIV).

These early followers obeyed Jesus' instructions, and His promise was fulfilled in their lives.

> When the day of Pentecost came, they were all together in one place. Suddenly . . . all of them were filled with the Holy Spirit and began to speak in other tongues as the Spirit enabled them *(2:1-2, 4, NIV)*.

Utterly amazed, the people who heard them asked, "How is it that each of us hears them . . . declaring the wonders of God in our own tongues?" *(vv. 8, 11, NIV)*.

## The Testimony of the Apostles

The gift of the sanctifying Spirit did not cease with the Day of Pentecost. Later when men were converted in Samaria, Peter and John came from Jerusalem. They themselves had received the Holy Spirit in the Upper Room on the Day of Pentecost. When they arrived in Samaria they prayed for the new Christians,

**TO BE HOLY IS TO BE WHOLE, AS GOD INTENDS HIS CHILD TO BE.**

> that they might receive the Holy Spirit, because the Holy Spirit had not yet come upon any of them; they had simply been baptized into the name of the Lord Jesus. Then Peter and John placed their hands on them, and they received the Holy Spirit *(8:15-17, NIV)*.

Saul of Tarsus met Christ on the road to Damascus. Chastened, and open to God's work in his spirit, he prayed in the house of Judas on Straight Street. There, a Spirit-led Ananias came to him and said,

> "Brother Saul, the Lord—Jesus, who appeared to you on the road as you were coming here—has sent me so that you may see again and be filled with the Holy Spirit." Immediately, something like scales fell from Saul's eyes, and he could see again *(9:17-18, NIV)*.

Seventeen years later the Lord's man was still proclaiming this uttermost salvation. When Paul found a small group of believers in Ephesus, his first question to them was, "Have ye received the Holy Ghost since ye believed?" They replied, "We have not so much as heard whether there be any Holy Ghost." To these sincere but untaught disciples Paul explained the connection between salvation and Christ's promise of the Holy Spirit. The Bible reports, "When they heard this, they were baptized in the name of the Lord Jesus. And when Paul had laid his hands on them, the Holy Ghost came on them" (19:5-6).

Three years still later the missionary writes to his Christian converts in northern Greece,

> The very God of peace sanctify you wholly; and I pray God your whole spirit and soul and body be preserved blameless unto the coming of our Lord Jesus Christ. Faithful is he that calleth you, who also will do it *(1 Thess. 5:23-24)*.

Stirred by the same concern for God's deeper ministry to His people, James admonishes his Jewish-Christian readers, "Draw nigh to God, and he will draw nigh to you. Cleanse your hands, ye sinners; and purify your hearts, ye double minded" (James 4:8).

John the Beloved was the last living apostle who had known Jesus personally. Remembering the teachings of our Lord, John assures us,

## A HOLY GOD DESIRES A HOLY PEOPLE.

> If we walk in the light, as he is in the light . . . the blood of Jesus Christ his Son cleanseth us from all sin. . . . If we confess our sins, he is faithful and just to forgive us our sins, and to cleanse us from all unrighteousness *(1 John 1:7, 9)*.

The message of Christian holiness thus finds many voices in the Bible. It is clear that a holy God desires a holy people. He makes His will known to us and shows us how we may open our lives to the coming of His Holy Spirit. Early in the Bible we hear God's expressed concern, "Sanctify yourselves, and ye shall be holy; for I am holy" (Lev. 11:44). In a final note from God's written revelation John exhorts the children of God, "Let him who is holy continue to be holy" (Rev. 22:11, NIV).

## THE FAITH WE BELIEVE

It is clear that the Bible places great importance on the teaching of holiness. Because that is so, the Church of the Nazarene places great emphasis on this truth. The opening words of the Church Constitution make our position clear:

> In order that we may preserve our God-given heritage, the faith once delivered to the saints, especially the doctrine and experience of entire sanctification as a second work of grace . . . we, the ministers and lay members of the Church of the Nazarene, . . . do hereby ordain, adopt, and set forth as the fundamental law or Constitution of the Church of the Nazarene the Articles of Faith.

All 16 Articles of Faith begin with the words "We believe." These are key words, for these doctrines are what we understand to be taught in the Word of God. Bible scholars have arranged these teachings systematically in order to state our doctrines clearly.

Article X gives our teaching on entire sanctification, which is the distinguishing doctrine of the Church of the Nazarene. It is given in two parts, paragraphs 13 and 14. Paragraph 13 reads as follows:

> We believe that entire sanctification is that act of God, subsequent to regeneration, by which believers are made free from original sin, or depravity, and brought into a state of entire devotement to God, and the holy obedience of love made perfect.
>
> It is wrought by the baptism with the Holy Spirit, and comprehends in

one experience the cleansing of the heart from sin and the abiding, indwelling presence of the Holy Spirit, empowering the believer for life and service.

Entire sanctification is provided by the blood of Jesus, is wrought instantaneously by faith, preceded by entire consecration; and to this work and state of grace the Holy Spirit bears witness.

This experience is also known by various terms representing its different phases, such as "Christian perfection," "perfect love," "heart purity," "the baptism with the Holy Spirit, "the fullness of the blessing," and "Christian holiness."

## Entire Sanctification

We use the term *sanctification* because it is a biblical term; it means "to make holy." We speak of *entire sanctification* because this second work of grace is not God's only action dealing with sin in human life. When our sins are forgiven, God imparts new spiritual life—we call it *regeneration*. We sometimes use the term *initial sanctification* because it is a first work of grace in which God begins to make us like himself.

Entire sanctification comes after we have been forgiven and regenerated. It is the work of God in which He cleanses original sin from the human spirit. Because of the fall of man, we are born into this world with an inclination to sin. It is natural to want our own way. Before self-centeredness has been cleansed, we are inclined to insist on our way even when it conflicts with God's way.

After we have been forgiven, this underlying spirit of wanting our own way is still present in the Christian. No person can do the will of God satisfactorily so long as he or she harbors a latent spirit of antagonism toward the plans of God. The opposition—every trace of it—needs to be cleansed. A person needs to be sanctified wholly. God promises to do this for us if we will let Him fill us with His own Spirit.

## Following Regeneration

We commonly speak of entire sanctification as a second definite work of grace. We believe that this is the way God gives the fullness of His Spirit to us.

THE EXPERIENCE OF THE CHURCH SUPPORTS THE EVIDENCE OF SCRIPTURE.

In the New Testament the call to holy living is most often addressed to those who are already followers of Christ. Jesus asked His disciples to tarry until the Holy Spirit came upon them. They obeyed Jesus' instructions and were baptized with the Holy Spirit. The apostles' exhortations to be sanctified and to be cleansed were addressed to Christian congregations in the Early Church.

The experience of the Church supports the evidence of Scripture. Almost without exception those who stress the work of the Holy Spirit stress the importance of a conscious seeking for His fullness. Those who testify to an assurance of being filled with the Spirit found this experience and this assurance as a significant crisis after they were converted. These testimonies come not only from within the holiness churches but also from Spirit-filled Christians in other groups.

From our knowledge of human nature we would expect God to deal with us in this sequence. In conversion we are normally thinking about our sins and our need for forgiveness. It is only after we have followed Christ for some time that we sense the need for a deeper relationship. We may discover unexpected attitudes of resistance to God's will. Or, we find ourselves yearning with the songwriter, "Into the love of Jesus, deeper I would go." It is these experiences of conviction and desire that open the door to conscious seeking. At the end of our obedient tarrying we discover a new dimension in our relationship with Christ. It is so outstanding that we can accurately describe it only as a second blessing, *subsequent to regeneration.*

## Devotion and Obedience

When the human spirit is cleansed from the sin of opposition, we are *brought into a state of entire devotement to God.* Here is the spirit that Jesus showed in Gethsemane when He prayed, "Father . . . everything is possible for you. Take this cup from me. Yet not what I will, but what you will" (Mark 14:36, NIV). Who can object to such full love for God? Who would find fault with such deep devotion to Christ?

This full acceptance of God's will for our lives is a *holy obedience.* It is an obedience based on *love made perfect.* But it is not an attitude that we can generate by ourselves. Such a spirit flows from a heart filled with God's love; a heart cleansed from self-seeking, and filled with a holy desire to do the whole will of God. This attitude comes from the fulfillment of the divine promise, "I will give you a new heart and put a new spirit in you. . . . I will put my Spirit in you and move you to follow my decrees and be careful to keep my laws" (Ezek. 36:26-27, NIV).

## Cleansing and Empowering

To be filled with the Holy Spirit is God's will for us and His gift to us. This is God's work—the work of the Father, Son, and Holy Spirit. In the first paragraph of our doctrinal statement we affirm that entire sanctification is an *act of God.* In paragraph three we state that it is *provided by the blood of Jesus.* In the second paragraph we affirm that *it is wrought by the baptism with the Holy Spirit.*

Jesus is our authority for identifying this experience chiefly with the work of the Holy Spirit. Our Lord promised to send the Comforter to His followers, and He told them what the coming of the Holy Spirit would do for them.

We believe that entire sanctification and the baptism with the Holy Spirit are the same work of God. Together they form one experience. When we are filled with the Holy Spirit, His presence cleanses all sin from our hearts. Filled with His love and power, we want nothing contrary to God's will for us. The instantaneous cleansing of entire sanctification is the result of His coming. Also God's indwelling Spirit continues to give strength to overcome evil around us; His presence gives us the desire and the strength to serve our Lord as witnesses.

### Several Names—One Reality

We often speak of entire sanctification as the baptism with the Holy Spirit because the Bible uses both terms to describe God's sanctifying work. It is only natural that we should thus find different ways of expressing God's ministry to our spirits. Among Christians we hear God's first work of salvation described in different terms. We speak of being *saved, converted, born again, justified,* and *regenerated.* Human life is beautifully varied, and God's ministries to us affect every aspect of life. It is natural, therefore, to describe His work of entire sanctification as we experience it. That is why we recognize that the reality of this experience may be expressed in different ways.

The terms *Christian perfection* and *perfect love* raise questions even among many who believe in Christian holiness. How can any human be perfect? How can anyone honestly profess that even His love is all that it could be?

The Bible nowhere teaches that we reach a point in Christlikeness in this life beyond which we cannot improve. By Christian perfection we mean only that it is possible to do what Jesus defined as God's will for us: "Thou shalt love the Lord thy God with all thy heart, and with all thy soul, and with all thy mind" (Matt. 22:37).

> OUR CREED AFFIRMS THAT JESUS DIED FOR OUR SANCTIFICATION.

It is possible to love God above all else, and in this sense to have a perfect love. It is possible to follow Christ as faithfully as we know how, and in this sense to satisfy Him completely—perfectly. He has given us His own Holy Spirit to inspire and enable us.

### Jesus Died to Sanctify Us

Our creed affirms that Jesus died for our sanctification just as truly as He died for the forgiveness of our sins: "Entire sanctification is provided by the blood of Jesus" (par. 13c). The Scripture says, "Wherefore Jesus also, that he might sanctify the people with his own blood, suffered without the gate" (Heb. 13:12). George Bennard reflects the truth of Scripture when he writes,

> For 'twas on that old Cross Jesus suffered and died
> To pardon and sanctify me.

### Sanctification Is a Crisis Experience

We believe that God sanctifies us in a moment of time, just as He saves us in an instant. Entire sanctification, like conversion, is thus a crisis experience.

We believe in instantaneous sanctification because that is the way it occurred in the Bible: "Suddenly . . . all of them were filled with the Holy Spirit" (Acts 2:2, 4, NIV). "Then laid they their hands on them, and they received the Holy Ghost" (8:17).

Sanctification can be an instant experience because faith is the human catalyst that permits the Holy Spirit to unite with our spirits. God's Spirit fills our spirits in a moment of choice—in an act of commitment and trust. In the instant that we exert saving faith, our sins are forgiven. In the moment that we exert sanctifying faith, the Holy Spirit comes in His fullness.

This union with the Spirit of Christ is so complete that Paul sometimes could scarcely determine the boundaries of his own transformed personality. He writes,

> I am crucified with Christ: nevertheless I live; yet not I, but Christ liveth in me: and the life which I now live in the flesh I live by the faith of the Son of God, who loved me, and gave himself for me *(Gal. 2:20).*

## The Place of Consecration

God cannot cleanse our spirits from any attitude that we withhold from Him. He will fill only those areas of our lives that we open to Him. Thus if we wish to be entirely sanctified, we must make an entire consecration. Paul urges,

> I plead with you therefore, brethren, by the compassion of God, to present all your faculties to Him as a living and holy sacrifice acceptable to Him . . . And . . . be transformed by the entire renewal of your minds, so that you may learn by experience what God's will is *(Rom. 12:1-2, WEYMOUTH).*

## We Can Be Sure

When we have made a full consecration, and are trusting God's promise to sanctify us, we may enjoy *the fullness of the blessing.* The *Manual* states our belief at this point: "To this work and state of grace the Holy Spirit bears witness" (par. 3c). We may know when we have been filled with the Spirit and sanctified wholly.

That is the way it happened in the New Testament. Peter knew that he and others had received the promised Holy Spirit on the Day of Pentecost. He had also seen the Holy Spirit given to Gentile converts in Samaria and in the house of Cornelius. When the Holy Spirit comes, He makes His presence known. Peter declares, "God, which knoweth the hearts, bare them witness, giving them the Holy Ghost, even as he did unto us; and put no difference between us and them, purifying their hearts by faith" (Acts 15:8-9).

John Wesley writes:

> By the testimony of the Spirit, I mean an inward impression on the soul, whereby the Spirit of God immediately and directly witnesses to my spirit that I am a child of God. The child of God can no more doubt this

evidence than he can doubt the shining of the sun while he stands in the full blaze of its beams.

Paul knew this deep inner assurance from God as he wrote, "When we cry, 'Abba! Father!', it is this Spirit testifying along with our own spirit that we are children of God" (Rom. 8:15-16, MOFFATT).

## A LIFE TO BE LIVED

God's work of entire sanctification begins in a crisis experience. The Holy Spirit comes in His fullness in a moment of time. But the work of that moment in purifying our hearts by faith, is the beginning of a lifelong process of developing mature Christian character.

**A HOLY LIFE IS NOT LIVED IN A MOMENT OF TIME.**

A holy life is not lived in a moment of time. It takes a lifetime to live a life. But when we have been sanctified wholly we have God's best provision to "serve him without fear, in holiness and righteousness . . . all the days of our life" (Luke 1:74-75).

This is the import of paragraph 14 of the *Manual,* which reads:

We believe that there is a marked distinction between a pure heart and a mature character. The former is obtained in an instant, the result of entire sanctification; the latter is the result of growth in grace.

We believe that the grace of entire sanctification includes the impulse to grow in grace. However, this impulse must be consciously nurtured, and careful attention given to the requisites and processes of spiritual development and improvement in Christlikeness of character and personality. Without such purposeful endeavor one's witness may be impaired and the grace itself frustrated and ultimately lost.

## Dealing with Failure

Can a sanctified Christian backslide? Yes. Jesus says clearly, "If a man abide not in me, he is cast forth as a branch, and is withered" (John 15:6). In all spiritual life, what can be received can be lost. It is possible to backslide completely after having been sanctified wholly. Paul warns, "Grieve not the holy Spirit of God" (Eph. 4:30). However, failure usually comes not because of some decisive act of rejection. Rather, there is a gradual, almost unnoticed lack of attention to the spiritual life. Through failure to abide in Christ, we wither.

Carelessness can cause the love of God in our souls to grow weak. When love is weakened, disregard is near. When we disregard God, we may next grieve Him away by blighting indifferences or by willful rebellion. The Holy Spirit does not remain where He is not made welcome, nor where His will is rejected.

If after we have been sanctified we become careless of our vows to God, or if we have not been as aggressive in the spiritual life as we should have been, what shall we do? Shall we, in our hours of awakening, throw away our confidence in all that God has done for us? Shall we assume that we are utterly backslidden and are now to begin entirely anew?

No. God is a God of steadfast love. He will not abandon us quickly. But we must cease to be careless or we shall eventually lose our souls. Let us ask God to forgive our neglect. Let us tarry until we are conscious again of His approval and the blessing of His presence. His promise is, "Draw near to God and he will draw near to you" (James 4:8, RSV).

## Grow Up into Christ

The goal of the sanctified Christian is Christlikeness. This is an endless quest; no one fully arrives. In seeking the goal of Christlikeness one can never be complacent. It involves listening daily to the promptings of the Holy Spirit within. It may require positive effort to do God's will sometimes when we may not particularly feel like it. But for the truly sanctified Christian, to know God's will as the Holy Spirit reveals it, is to do it.

The purpose of Spirit-filled Christians is to live all of life as Christ would want us to live—for as long as we live. Paul voices this longing and commitment for every Spirit-filled Christian: "We will in all things grow up into him who is the Head, that is, Christ. From him the whole body . . . grows and builds itself up in love, as each part does its work" (Eph. 4:15-16, NIV).

## MY GLAD WITNESS

As a young Christian beginning my junior year in college, I felt a deep need to be cleansed from sin and to be filled with the Holy Spirit. I knelt at the altar in a college chapel and earnestly sought this blessing. At the altar God graciously dealt with my soul and helped me to reach a place of utter commitment to Him, but the assurance of full salvation did not come immediately. I sought on for a day or two. One morning in my dormitory room as I knelt by the window in meditation and prayer, it happened. Just as the first rays of the rising sun touched the building and lighted up my windowpane, the Holy Spirit came to my soul and illuminated all of my life.

I cannot yet testify to the end of my days, but I can testify that for these years He has been with me. There have been some days of uncertainty, but He has remained faithful. He has made me a better man than I was then. He has led me into paths of Christian service of which I did not dream. The prospect has not always been bright, but looking back the path has always been radiant with the joy of His companionship. In the light of this faith, and with the assurance of His sanctifying presence, I propose to journey until traveling days are done.

Originally published as chapter 4 of *Growing Up in Christ: for Serious Disciples,* Neil B. Wiseman, ed. (Kansas City: Nazarene Publishing House, 1991), 57-71.

After interviewing 652
members of the society
who were exceeding clear
in their experience,
and of whose testimony
I could see no reason to doubt . . .
all who believe they are sanctified
declare with one voice
that the change
was wrought in a moment.
I cannot but believe that
sanctification is commonly,
if not always,
an instantaneous work.

—John Wesley

From "Sermon: On Patience," in *Great Holiness Classics,* Vol. 2: *The Wesley Century,* T. Crichton Mitchell, ed. (Kansas City: Beacon Hill Press of Kansas City, 1984), 147.

# 2

# WHAT WESLEY TAUGHT ABOUT HOLINESS
## —Two Works of Grace—

## John Wesley

NOT LONG AFTER, I think in the spring, 1741, we published a second volume of hymns. As the doctrine was still misunderstood, and consequently misrepresented, I judged it needful to explain yet farther upon the head; which was done in the preface to it as follows:

This great gift of God, the salvation of our souls, is no other than the image of God fresh stamped on our hearts. It is a "renewal of believers in the spirit of their minds, after the likeness of Him that created them." God hath now laid "the axe unto the root of the tree, purifying their hearts by faith," and "cleansing all the thoughts of their hearts by the inspiration of His Holy Spirit." Having this hope, that they shall see God as He is, they "purify themselves even as He is pure," and are "holy, as He that hath called them is holy, in all manner of conversation." Not that they have already attained all that they shall attain, either are already in this sense perfect. But they daily "go on from strength to strength, beholding" now, "as in a glass, the glory of the Lord, they are changed into the same image, from glory to glory, by the Spirit of the Lord."

And "where the Spirit of the Lord is, there is liberty"; such liberty "from the law of sin and death," as the children of this world will not believe, though a man declare it unto them. "The Son hath made them free," who are thus "born of God," from that great root of sin and bitterness, pride. They feel that all their "sufficiency is of God," that it is He alone who "is in all their thoughts," and "worketh in them both to will and to do of His good pleasure." They feel that "it is not they" that "speak, but the Spirit of" their "Father who speaketh" in them, and that whatsoever is done by their hands, "the Father who is in them, He doeth the works." So that God is to them all in all, and they are nothing in His sight. They are freed from self-will, as desiring nothing but the holy and perfect will of God: not supplies in want, not ease in pain,[1] nor life, or death, or any creature; but continually crying in their inmost soul, "Father, Thy will be done." They are freed from evil thoughts, so that they cannot enter into them, no, not for a moment. Aforetime, when an evil thought came in, they looked up, and it vanished away. But now it does not come in, there being no room for this, in a soul which is full of God. They are free from wanderings in prayer. Whensoever they pour out their hearts in a more immediate manner before God, they have no thought of anything past[2] or absent, or to come, but of God alone. In times past, they had wandering thoughts darting in, which yet fled away like smoke; but now that smoke does not rise at all. They have no fear or doubt, either is to their state in general, or as to any particular action.[3] The "unction from the Holy one" teacheth them every hour what they shall do, and what they shall speak;[4] nor, therefore, have they any need to reason concerning it.[5] They are in one sense freed from temptations; for though numberless temptations fly about them, yet they trouble them not.[6] At all times their souls are even and calm, their hearts are steadfast and unmovable. Their peace, flowing as a river, "passeth all understanding," and they "rejoice with joy unspeakable and full of glory." For they "are sealed by the Spirit unto the day of redemption," having the witness in themselves, that there is laid up for them a "crown of righteousness, which the Lord will give" them "in that day."[7]

Not that every one is a child of the devil, till he is thus renewed in love; on the contrary, whoever has "a sure confidence in God, that, through the merits of Christ, his sins are forgiven," he is a child of God, and, if he abide in Him, an heir of all the promises. Neither ought he in any wise to cast away his confidence, or to deny the faith he has received, because it is weak, or because it is "tried with fire," so that his soul is "in heaviness through manifold temptations."

Neither dare we affirm, as some have done, that all this salvation is given at once. There is, indeed, an instantaneous, as well as a gradual work of God in His children; and there wants not, we know, a cloud of witnesses, who have received, in one moment, either a clear sense of the forgiveness of their sins, or the abiding witness of the Holy Spirit. But we do not know a single instance, in any place, of a person's receiving, in one and the same moment, remission of sins, the abiding witness of the Spirit, and a new, clean heart.

Indeed, how God may work, we cannot tell; but the general manner wherein He does work, is this: those who once trusted in themselves that they were righteous, that they were rich, and increased in goods, and had need of nothing, are, by the Spirit of God applying His word, convinced that they are poor and naked. All the things that they have done are brought to their remembrance and set in array before them, so that they see the wrath of God hanging over their heads, and feel that they deserve the damnation of hell. In their trouble they cry unto the Lord, and He shows them that He hath taken away their sins, and opens the kingdom of Heaven in their hearts,—"righteousness, and peace, and joy in the Holy Ghost." Sorrow and pain are fled away, and "sin has no more dominion over" them. Knowing they are justified freely through faith in His blood, they "have peace with God through Jesus Christ"; they "rejoice in hope of the glory of God," and "the love of God is shed abroad in their hearts."

In this peace they remain for days, or weeks, or months, and commonly suppose they shall not know war any more; till some of their old enemies, their bosom sins, or the sin which did most easily beset them (perhaps anger or desire), assault them again, and thrust sore at them, that they may fall. Then arises fear that they shall not endure to the end; and often doubt whether God has not forgotten them, or whether they did not deceive themselves in thinking their sins were forgiven. Under these clouds, especially if they reason with the devil, they go mourning all the day long. But it is seldom long before their Lord answers for Himself, sending them the Holy Ghost to comfort them, to bear witness continually with their spirits that they are the children of God. Then they are, indeed, meek, and gentle, and teachable, even as a little child.

And now first do they see the ground of their heart,[8] which God before would not disclose unto them, lest the soul should fail before Him, and the spirit which He had made. Now they see all the hidden abominations there, the depths of pride, self-will, and hell; yet having the witness in themselves, "Thou art an heir of God, a joint heir with Christ, even in the midst of this fiery trial"; which continually heightens both the strong sense they then have of their inability to help themselves, and the inexpressible hunger they feel after a full renewal in His image, in "righteousness and true holiness."

Then God is mindful of the desire of them that fear Him, and gives them a single eye, and a pure heart; He stamps upon them His own image and superscription; He createth them anew in Christ Jesus; He cometh unto them with His Son and blessed Spirit, and, fixing His abode in their souls, bringeth them into the "rest which remaineth for the people of God."

Here I cannot but remark, (1) That this is the strongest account we ever gave of Christian perfection—indeed, too strong in more than one particular, as is observed in the notes annexed. (2) That there is nothing which we have since advanced upon the subject, either in verse or prose, which is not either directly or indirectly contained in this preface. So that whether our present doctrine be right or wrong, it is, however, the same which we taught from the beginning.

## THE REST THAT REMAINS

I need not give additional proofs of this, by multiplying quotations from the volume itself. It may suffice to cite part of one hymn only, the last in that volume:

*Lord, I believe a rest remains,*
  *To all Thy people known;*
*A rest where pure enjoyment reigns,*
  *And thou art loved alone;*

*A rest where all our soul's desire*
  *Is fixed on things above;*
*Where doubt and pain and fear expire,*
  *Cast out by perfect love.*

*From every evil motion freed*
  *(The Son hath made us free,)*
*On all the powers of hell we tread,*
  *In glorious liberty.*

*Safe in the way of life, above*
  *Death, earth, and hell we rise;*
*We find, when perfected in love,*
  *Our long-sought paradise.*

*Oh, that I now the rest might know,*
  *Believe and enter in!*
*Now, Saviour, now the power bestow,*
  *And let me cease from sin!*

*Remove this hardness from my heart,*
  *This unbelief remove;*
*To me the rest of faith impart,*
  *The sabbath of Thy love.*

*Come, O my Saviour, come away!*
  *Into my soul descend!*
*No longer from Thy creature stay,*
  *My author and my end.*

*The bliss Thou hast for me prepared,*
  *No longer be delayed;*
*Come, my exceeding great reward,*
  *For whom I first was made.*

> *Come Father, Son, and Holy Ghost,*
> *And seal me Thine abode!*
> *Let all I am in Thee be lost;*
> *Let all be lost in God!*

Can anything be more clear than, (1) That here, also, is as full and high a salvation as we have ever spoken of? (2) That this is spoken of as receivable by mere faith, and as hindered only by unbelief? (3) That this faith, and consequently the salvation which it brings, is spoken of as given in an instant? (4) That it is supposed that instant may be now? That we need not stay another moment? That "now," the very "now is the accepted time? Now is the day of" this full "salvation"? And, lastly, that, if any speak otherwise, he is the person that brings new doctrine among us?

## MISUNDERSTANDINGS CONCERNING PERFECTION

About a year after, namely, in the year 1742, we published another volume of hymns. The dispute being now at the height, we spoke upon the head more largely than ever before. Accordingly, abundance of the hymns in this volume treat expressly on this subject. And so does the preface, which, as it is short, it may not be amiss to insert entire:

(1) Perhaps the general prejudice against Christian perfection may chiefly arise from a misapprehension of the nature of it. We willingly allow and continually declare, there is no such perfection in this life, as implies either a dispensation from doing good, and attending all the ordinances of God, or a freedom from ignorance, mistake, temptation, and a thousand infirmities necessarily connected with flesh and blood.

(2) First, we not only allow, but earnestly contend, that there is no perfection in this life, which implies any dispensation from attending all the ordinances of God, or from doing good unto all men while we have time, though "especially unto the household of faith." We believe, that not only the babes in Christ, who have newly found redemption in His blood, but those also who are "grown up into perfect men," are indispensably obliged, as often as they have opportunity, "to eat bread and drink wine in remembrance of Him," and to "search the Scriptures"; by fasting, as well as temperance, to "keep their bodies under, and bring them into subjection"; and, above all, to pour out their souls in prayer, both secretly, and in the great congregation.

(3) We secondly believe that there is no such perfection in this life, as implies an entire deliverance, either from ignorance, or mistake, in things not essential to salvation, or from manifold temptations, or from numberless infirmities, wherewith the corruptible body more or less presses down the soul. We cannot find any ground in Scripture to suppose, that any inhabitant of a house of clay is wholly exempt either from bodily infirmities,

or from ignorance of many things; or to imagine any is incapable of mistake, or failing into divers temptations.

(4) But whom, then, do you mean by "one that is perfect"? We mean one in whom is "the mind which was in Christ," and who so "walketh as Christ also walked"; a man "that hath clean hands and a pure heart," or that is "cleansed from all filthiness of flesh and spirit"; one in whom is "no occasion of stumbling," and who, accordingly, "does not commit sin." To declare this a little more particularly: we understand by that Scriptural expression, "a perfect man," one in whom God hath fulfilled His faithful word, "From all your filthiness and from all your idols I will cleanse you: I will also save you from all your uncleannesses." We understand, hereby, one whom God hath "sanctified throughout in body, soul, and spirit"; one who "walketh in the light as He is in the light, in whom is no darkness at all; the blood of Jesus Christ His Son having cleansed him from all sin."

(5) This man can now testify to all mankind, "I am crucified with Christ: nevertheless I live; yet not I but Christ liveth in me." He is "holy as God who called" him "is holy,'" both in heart and "in all manner of conversation." He "loveth the Lord his God with all his heart," and serveth him "with all his strength." He "loveth his neighbor," every man, "as himself"; yea, "as Christ loveth us"; them, in particular, that "despitefully use him and persecute him, because they know not the Son, neither the Father." Indeed, his soul is all love, filled with "bowels of mercies, kindness, meekness, gentleness, long-suffering." And his life agreeth thereto, full of "the work of faith, the patience of hope, the labor of love." "And whatsoever" he "doeth either in word or deed," he "doeth it all in the name," in the love and power "of the Lord Jesus." In a word, he doeth "the will of God on earth, as it is done in heaven."

(6) This it is to be a perfect man, to be "sanctified throughout"; even "to have a heart so all-flaming with the love of God" (to use Archbishop Ussher's words), "as continually to offer up every thought, word, and work, as a spiritual sacrifice, acceptable to God through Christ." In every thought of our hearts, in every word of our tongues, in every work of our hands, to "show forth His praise, who hath called us out of darkness into His marvelous light." O that both we, and all who seek the Lord Jesus in sincerity, may thus "be made perfect in one!"

This is the doctrine which we preached from the beginning, and which we preach at this day. Indeed, by viewing it in every point of light, and comparing it again and again with the word of God on the one hand, and the experience of the children of God on the other, we saw farther into the nature and properties of Christian perfection. But still there is no contrariety at all between our first and our last sentiments. Our first conception of it was, "It is to have 'the mind which was in Christ,'" and to "walk as He walked"; to have all the mind that was in Him, and always to walk as He walked: in other words, to be inwardly and outwardly devoted to God; all devoted in heart and life. And we have the same conception of it now, without either addition or diminution.

## QUESTIONS AND ANSWERS ON THE DOCTRINE OF SANCTIFICATION

On Monday, June 25, 1744, our first conference began; six clergymen and all our preachers being present. The next morning we seriously considered the doctrine of sanctification, or perfection. The questions asked concerning it, and the substance of the answers given were as follows:

*What is it to be sanctified?*
To be renewed in the image of God, "in righteousness and true holiness."

*What is implied in being a perfect Christian?*
The loving God with all our heart, and mind, and soul (Deut. 6:5).

*Does this imply that all inward sin is taken away?*
Undoubtedly; or how can we be said to be "saved from all our uncleannesses"? (Ezek. 36:29).

Our second conference began August 1, 1745. The next morning we spoke of sanctification as follows: —

*When does inward sanctification begin?*
In the moment a man is justified. (Yet sin remains in him, yea, the seed of all sin, till he is sanctified throughout.) From that time a believer gradually dies to sin, and grows in grace.

*Is this ordinarily given till a little before death?*
It is not, to those who expect it no sooner.

*But may we expect it sooner?*
Why not? For, although we grant,
(1) that the generality of believers, whom we have hitherto known, were not so sanctified till near death;
(2) that few of those to whom St. Paul wrote his Epistles were so at that time; nor,
(3) he himself at the time of writing his former Epistles; yet all this does not prove, that we may not be so today.

*In what manner should we preach sanctification?*
Scarce at all to those who are not pressing forward; to those who are, always by way of promise; always drawing, rather than driving.

Our third conference began Tuesday, May 26, 1746. In this we carefully read over the minutes of the two preceding conferences, to observe whether anything contained therein might be retrenched or altered on more mature consideration. But we did not see cause to alter in any respect what we had agreed upon before.

Our fourth conference began on Tuesday, June the 16th, 1747. As several persons were present, who did not believe the doctrine of perfection, we agreed to examine it from the foundation.

In order to this, it was asked,

**How much is allowed by our brethren who differ from us with regard to entire sanctification?**

They grant,

(1) That every one must be entirely sanctified in the article of death.

(2) That till then, a believer daily grows in grace, comes nearer and nearer to perfection.

(3) That we ought to be continually pressing after it, and to exhort all others so to do.

**What do we allow them?**

We grant,

(1) That many of those who have died in the faith, yea, the greater part of those we have known, were not perfected in love, till a little before their death.

(2) That the term *sanctified,* is continually applied by St. Paul, to all that were justified.

(3) That by this term alone, he rarely, if ever, means, "saved from all sin."

(4) That, consequently, it is not proper to use it in that sense, without adding the word *wholly, entirely,* or the like.

(5) That the inspired writers almost continually speak of, or to, those who were justified, but very rarely of, or to, those who were wholly sanctified.[9]

(6) That, consequently, it behooves us to speak almost continually of the state of justification; but more rarely,[10] "at least in full and explicit terms, concerning entire sanctification."

**What, then, is the point where we divide?**

It is this: should we expect to be saved from all sin before the article of death?

**Is there any clear Scripture promise of this, — that God will save us from all sin?**

There is: "He shall redeem Israel from all his sins" (Ps. 130:8).

This is more largely expressed in the prophecy of Ezekiel: "Then will I sprinkle clean water upon you, and ye shall be clean; from all your filthiness, and from all your idols, will I cleanse you; I will also save you from all your uncleannesses" (36:25, 29). No promise can be more clear. And to this the Apostle plainly refers in that exhortation: "Having these promises, let us cleanse ourselves from all filthiness of flesh and spirit, perfecting holiness in the fear of God" (2 Cor. 7:1). Equally clear and express is that ancient promise: "The Lord thy God will circumcise thy heart, and the heart of thy seed, to love the Lord thy God with all thy heart and with all thy soul" (Deut. 30:6).

### But does any assertion answerable to this, occur in the New Testament?

There does and that laid down in the plainest terms. So 1 John 3:8: "For this purpose the Son of God was manifested, that He might destroy the works of the devil"; the works of the devil, without any limitation or restriction; but all sin is the work of the devil. Parallel to which, is the assertion of St. Paul: "Christ loved the Church, and gave Himself for it, that He might present it to Himself, a glorious Church, not having spot or wrinkle, or any such thing, but that it might be holy and without blemish" (Eph. 5:25-27).

And to the same effect is his assertion in the eighth of the Romans, verses 3-4: "God sent His Son, that the righteousness of the law might be fulfilled in us, who walk not after the flesh, but after the Spirit."

### Does the New Testament afford any further ground for expecting to be saved from all sin?

Undoubtedly it does; both in those prayers and commands, which are equivalent to the strongest assertions.

### What prayers do you mean?

Prayers for entire sanctification; which, were there no such thing, would be mere mockery of God. Such, in particular, are

(1) "Deliver us from evil." Now, when this is done, when we are delivered from all evil, there can be no sin remaining.

(2) "Neither pray I for these alone, but for them also who shall believe on Me through their word; that they all may be one; as Thou, Father, art in Me, and I in Thee, that they also may be one in us; I in them, and Thou in Me, that they may be made perfect in one'" (John 17:20-23).

(3) "I bow my knees unto the God and Father of our Lord Jesus Christ, that He would grant you, that ye, being rooted and grounded in love, may be able to comprehend, with all saints, what is the breadth, and length, and depth, and height, and to know the love of Christ, which passeth knowledge; that ye may be filled with all the fullness of God" (Eph. 3:14, etc.).

(4) "The very God of peace sanctify you wholly. And I pray God, your whole spirit, soul, and body, may be preserved blameless unto the coming of our Lord Jesus Christ" (1 Thess. 5:23).

**What command is there to the same effect?**
(1) "Be ye perfect, as your Father who is in heaven, is perfect" (Matt. 5:48).
(2) "Thou shalt love the Lord thy God with all thy heart, and with all thy soul, and with all thy mind" (Matt. 22:37). But if the love of God fill all the heart, there can be no sin therein.

**But how does it appear that this is to be done before the article of death?**
(1) From the very nature of a command, which is not given to the dead, but to the living. Therefore, "Thou shalt love God with all thy heart," cannot mean "Thou shalt do this when thou diest," but, while thou livest.
(2) From express texts of Scripture:
    (a) "The grace of God, that bringeth salvation, hath appeared to all men; teaching us that, having renounced ungodliness and worldly lusts, we should live soberly, righteously, and godly in this present world; looking for the glorious appearing of our Lord Jesus Christ, who gave Himself for us, that He might redeem us from all iniquity, and purify unto Himself a peculiar people, zealous of good works" (Titus 2:11-14);
    (b) "He hath raised up a horn of salvation for us, to perform the mercy promised to our fathers; the oath which He sware to our father Abraham, that He would grant unto us, that we, being delivered out of the hands of our enemies, should serve Him without fear, in holiness and righteousness before Him, all the days of our life" (Luke 1:69, etc.).

**Is there any example in Scripture, of persons who had attained to this?**
Yes; St. John, and all those of whom he says, "Herein is our love made perfect, that we may have boldness in the day of judgment; because, as He is, so are we in this world" (1 John 4:17).

**Can you show one such example now? Where is he that is thus perfect?**
To some that make this inquiry, one might answer, If I knew one here, I would not tell you; for you do not enquire out of love. You are like Herod; you only seek the young child to slay it.

But more directly we answer: There are many reasons why there should be few, if any, indisputable examples. What inconveniences would this bring on the person himself, set as a mark for all to shoot at! And how unprofitable would it be to gainsayers! "For if they hear not Moses and the Prophets," Christ and His Apostles, "neither would they be persuaded though one rose from the dead."

**Are we not apt to have a secret distaste to any who say they are saved from all sin?**
It is very possible we may, and that upon several grounds; partly from a concern for the good of souls, who may be hurt if these are not what they profess; partly from a kind of implicit envy at those who speak of higher attainments than our own; and partly from our natural slowness and unreadiness of heart to believe the works of God.

**Why may we not continue in the joy of faith, till we are perfected in love?**
Why indeed? Since holy grief does not quench this joy; since even while we are under the cross, while we deeply partake of the sufferings of Christ, we may rejoice with joy unspeakable.

From these extracts, it undeniably appears, not only what was mine and my brother's judgment, but what was the judgment of all the preachers in connection with us, in the years 1744, 45, 46, and 47. Nor do I remember that, in any one of these conferences, we had one dissenting voice; but whatever doubts any one had when we met, they were all removed before we parted.

---

1. This is too strong. Our Lord Himself desired ease in pain. He asked for it only with resignation: "Not as I will," I desire, "But as Thou wilt."

2. This is far too strong. See the sermon "On Wandering Thoughts."

3. Frequently this is the case; but only for a time.

4. For a time it may be so; but not always.

5. Sometimes they have no need; at other times they have.

6. Sometimes they do not; at other times they do, and that grievously.

7. Not all who are saved from sin; many of them have not attained it yet.

8. Is it not astonishing, that while this book is extant, which was published four and twenty years ago, any one should face me down, that this is new doctrine, and what I never taught before?

9. That is, unto those alone, exclusive of others; but they speak to them jointly with others, almost continually.

10. More rarely, I allow; but yet in some places, very frequently, strongly, and explicitly.

Excerpted from *A Plain Account of Christian Perfection* (Kansas City: Beacon Hill Press of Kansas City, 1966), 28-47.

Putting on Christ . . .

is not one among

many jobs a Christian

has to do;

and it is not a sort of

special exercise

for the top class.

It is the whole of

Christianity.

—C. S. Lewis

From *The Quotable Lewis,* Wayne Martindale and Jerry Root, eds. (Wheaton: Tyndale House Publishers, Inc., 1989), 92.

# 3

# WESLEY'S RELIGION IN JEFFERSON'S AMERICA
## —HOLINESS EVANGELISM AND THE METHODIST PURPOSE IN NORTH AMERICA—

## Timothy L. Smith

UNDER THE LEADERSHIP of John and Charles Wesley, a religious tradition emerged in 18th-century England that was a sufficiently new combination of Christian ideas, practices, and institutional forms as to constitute a distinct religious culture. Though rooted deeply in Anglicanism, Wesleyan religion drew explicitly upon other broad aspects of Protestant, Roman Catholic, and patristic traditions, and upon the Hebrew experience that lay behind the New Testament. This dependence was so close as to make plausible its claim to be a revival of primitive Christianity.

John Wesley's acknowledged indebtedness to Martin Luther, John Calvin, the English Puritans, and his close associations with Moravian Pietists reinforced that claim. In language entirely familiar to those who heard it, Wesley's movement offered easy points of entry to persons of diverse backgrounds. Yet clearly its synthesis of old doctrines and new forms and practices distinguished it sharply from other religious cultures of the period. Wesley believed he had drawn out of the Bible, in a decade or so of sustained and shared study, the essence of what humanity required and God had provided to secure individual salvation and moral order. That experience of faith brought deliverance from sin. Those who became Methodists sensed they were undergoing a profound conversion in perceptions and behavior.

Methodist culture in North America was a continuation of that which had taken shape a generation or two earlier in Oxford, London, and Bristol. By the eve of the American Revolution, when Methodist preachers first appeared in the New World, both the substance and the style of the Wesleyan way were so internally consistent as to be exportable to America without significant alteration. The founder's influence and authority were decisive during the following decades, despite the great distances, the disruptions brought on by the War for Independence, the early conversion of numbers of Blacks and Pennsylvania Germans, and the emerging myths and ideologies of a new nation.

In retrospect, the purpose and actual function of Methodist organization in North America were the same as those of Wesley's in England: Holiness evangelism. Methodism was geared to persuading men and women, especially the poor, to believe that the gospel promise of salvation from sin was to all and not simply to an elect few. By repentance and faith in Christ, ordinary sinners could be made holy and happy and lead human society toward justice. Both preachers and lay leaders adopted as their own the mission Wesley had laid upon the British Methodists: "to reform the nation, and spread scriptural holiness over these lands."

**HOLINESS MEANT THE RENUNCIATION OF ALL CLAIMS TO SPECIAL PRIVILEGES AND A COMMITMENT TO LOVE GOD AND SERVE THE POOR AND OPPRESSED.**

The moral intensity of this Wesleyan ideology was apparent everywhere in the United States during the years between 1775 and 1840. Methodists perceived the young nation's mission in international terms from the outset. Just as individual repentance and salvation followed the conviction of God's judgment upon sin, so must America's quest for a virtuous republic require the same. The mark of that repentance, they believed, was not self-indulgent nationalism, whether British or American. Holiness meant the renunciation of all claims to special privileges and a commitment to love God and serve the poor and oppressed. Methodist millennial rhetoric, which blossomed increasingly in the United States after 1800, echoed the teachings of Wesley and Fletcher; and the millennium these two had proclaimed was "a state of general holiness." Here, of course, Wesleyans shared a view that had come down also from Jonathan Edwards and the Puritans through Samuel Hopkins to Charles G. Finney.

American Methodism's democratically structured and expansively ideological culture did not for many decades shed its English, indeed its Anglican, pervading atmosphere. The first converts in and around Philadelphia and from Delaware and Maryland south were Anglicans, as were the Germans from Northern Ireland in Barbara Heck's circle in New York City. This created grave problems during the War for Independence, both for individuals and congregations. All suffered when patriot enthusiasts, reasoning from Wesley's ill-considered tract against the rebellion, spread the word that Methodists were Tories.

Francis Asbury, nevertheless, emerged from the experience an American patriot and eventually became, like most other Methodists in the country, a Jeffersonian republican. The substance as well as the rhetoric of Asbury's theology and preaching, however, remained thoroughly British. So with Anglican sacramental rituals and customs, Methodists baptized the infant children of their members, took the Lord's Supper at the kneeling rail, and departed from both services with the cadences of *The Book of Common Prayer* ringing in their ears.

Literature, as always with Methodists, was crucial to religious culture. The two short series of Asbury's *American Monthly* promoted the doctrine and experience of Christian perfection precisely as Wesley's *Arminian Magazine* in England did, often reprinting its materials. Testimonies, letters, and memorial sketches, including selections from Wesley's correspondence from the 1760s, described instantaneous experiences of being filled "with all His fullness of love" and "cleansed from all sinful tempers."

The third of the series of Wesley's later sermons published in the 1789 volume was his "The End of Christ's Coming," first printed in the English journal only four years before. It proclaimed the renewal of humanity in the "righteousness and holiness" that was the true image of God. "Be not content with any religion," the sermon urged, "which does not imply the destruction of all the works of the devil, that is, of all sin." The opening issue of the 1797 volume carried as its lead article Wesley's tract "The Character of a Methodist," which he had cited in the *Plain Account* to demonstrate his early commitment to Christian perfection.

Six months later Asbury reprinted one of Wesley's most explicit sermons on the experience of holiness of heart taken from the text of James 1:4: "Let patience have her perfect work, that ye may be perfect and entire, wanting nothing." What the second work of grace yielded, Wesley wrote, was not a "new kind of holiness"; to Christians in all stages of saving grace, "love is the fulfilling of the law" and "the sum of Christian sanctification." Rather, he explained, every true believer grows in faith and love, and thus, in holiness, "till it pleases God, after he is thoroughly convinced . . . of the total corruption of his nature, to take it all away; to purify his heart and cleanse him from all unrighteousness." And he urged his readers to seek that instant of cleansing "by plain, simple faith."

The influence of John and Charles Wesley upon the first three generations of American Holiness writings is not surprising. But the equally early influence of their colleague John Fletcher is not so well known. Indeed, pioneer American Methodists reprinted an imposing quantity of Fletcher's writings. During the years 1791 to 1795 alone, these included his complete *Works,* in five volumes; his *Appeal to Matters of Fact and Common Sense* (of which 12 more editions appeared between 1802 and 1840); his *Spiritual Letters;* his *Posthumous Pieces,* published in England only two years earlier, which included many of his letters on being filled with the Holy Spirit; and the account of his life by his wife, Mary. Five more American editions of Fletcher's complete *Works* appeared in the following decades, a second in 1809 and four more between 1833 and

1837, along with three editions of his intensely perfectionist *Portrait of St. Paul,* in 1804 and again in 1830 and 1834. Two editions of his brief editions of *Address to Imperfect Believers Who Cordially Embrace the Doctrine of Gospel Sanctification* were published in 1821 and 1829. Five of his classic group of seven volumes called *Checks to Antinomianism* appeared in 1819, 1820, 1828, and 1837.

> CHRISTIAN
> PERFECTION IN
> WESLEY'S VIEW,
> FLETCHER HAD SAID,
> IS NOTHING ELSE BUT
> "CHRIST, THROUGH
> THE HOLY SPIRIT,
> 'DWELLING IN OUR
> HEARTS BY FAITH.'"

The publication in America of two new editions of Wesley's *Works* (in 1826 and 1831) and four of John Fletcher's (between 1833 and 1837) provided rich additions to the material on heart purity long available in the widely circulated editions of the founder's *Sermons* and Fletcher's *Checks to Antinomianism.*

A review of Fletcher's *Works* published in the *Methodist Magazine* in October 1833 quoted at length his description of what Wesley contended for: "loving God with all our hearts, and our neighbor as ourselves" through "perfect love shed abroad in our hearts by the Holy Ghost given unto us." Christian perfection in Wesley's view, Fletcher had said, is nothing else but "Christ, through the Holy Spirit, 'dwelling in our hearts by faith,'" Christ "fully formed in our hearts." It represents "the fulfillment of the promise of the Father, that is, the gift of the Holy Spirit . . . to make us abound in righteousness, peace, and joy, through believing . . . it is the Shekinah, filling the Lord's human temple with glory."

Other important English Methodist teachers of the American churches were Hester Ann Rogers, whose journal and correspondence became staple fare for men and women seeking Christian holiness. Then Adam Clarke's published sermons and his commentary on the Bible circulated widely in North America. Also, Richard Watson became the most popular summarizer of Wesleyan theology on both sides of the Atlantic.

Under such compelling influences the message and experience took hold in the American church from its very beginnings. Asbury's diary and correspondence contain ample evidence of his own seeking and preaching the same experience. The decade of the 1790s saw no diminishing of the emphasis upon holiness of heart and life. Richard Whatcoat recorded the numbers of persons "justified" and those "sanctified" at his meetings in 1789 and 1790. He used these code words in the same manner Wesley had used them since at least 1761. The ninth edition of the *Pocket Hymnbook* published in 1789, though labeled as "collected from various authors," contained chiefly hymns by John and Charles Wesley. Among them were long-popular petitions for holiness of heart, such as the one now known by what was then the opening of the third stanza of the hymn "Jesus, Thine All-Victorious Love." Another began, "Lord, I believe a rest remains / To all thy people known."

In 1796 the fourth and earliest extant edition of the catechism prepared "for the use of Methodist societies" contained clear but simple answers, consisting chiefly of Scripture quotations and basic questions on the Fall, free grace, a universal atonement, the nature of saving faith, the witness of the Spirit, empowerment by grace to obey God's law, and the duty of Christians to aid the poor.

Especially notable in that catechism, however, is Lesson 13. The question is, "Has God promised to do anything more for faithful Christians in this life?" The reply was one of Wesley's favorite Old Testament texts that he believed promised entire sanctification, Ezek. 36:25-26. To the question "On what conditions may Christians expect to be sanctified wholly?" the answer was, in the words of 1 John 1:7, "If we walk in the light, as he is in the light, we have fellowship one with another, and the blood of Jesus Christ his Son cleanseth us from all sin." Six succeeding questions all bore answers drawn from the litany of New Testament texts that Wesley had first laid out in support of the doctrine of Christian holiness 50 years earlier. Constant instruction and repetition had made them the focus of Methodist religious consciousness.

Little wonder that, sustained by such resources, ministers preached entire sanctification with great assurance. One who had been recently assigned to the maritime provinces of Canada wrote in 1797 that after a love feast he "never saw or heard more witnesses profess perfect love, according to the number of people." Coke and Asbury, in their "Notes" attached to the *Book of Discipline* for 1798, declared that preachers must "lead the lambs and sheep of Christ." Not sparing "the remaining man of sin," they must hold Christ forth "as 'able to save them to the uttermost that come unto God by Him.'" They must "describe to them in all its richest views, the blessing of perfect love," showing how Christ "is *this moment* able and willing to reduce the mountain into a plain."

Similar testimony appeared as Methodism spread to new areas. In Charleston, South Carolina, Edgar Wells, a merchant, was converted during Asbury's first preaching there in 1785. He soon became "deeply convinced of inbred sin, and the great necessity of holiness of heart, and of enjoying the fullness of perfect love." For Wells' last three years of his life, a report in the *Methodist Magazine* for 1797 tells us he enjoyed "the witness" of the Spirit to this experience and testified to "constant communion with God."

In 1788 one of three traveling ministers in Wilkes County, Georgia, wrote that among the 3,000 Methodist converts won there during the preceding three years, "the work of sanctification goes on sweetly and powerfully."

From the Cumberland Mountains of Kentucky and Tennessee, elder James Haw wrote Asbury in 1789 that recent quarterly conferences, drawing together preachers from numerous circuits and laypersons from nearby, were occasions when "the Lord poured out His Spirit in wonderful manner, first on the Christians, sanctifying some of them very powerfully and gloriously, and as I charitably hope, wholly. Typically, Haw wrote, "The work of sanctification amongst believers broke out at the Lord's table," prompting deep conviction and repentance among unbelievers present. In the Cumberland Circuit he reported, "We have 112 disciples now . . . 47 of whom, I trust, have received the gift of the Holy Ghost since they believed."

The immense expansion of Methodism that followed in America during the presidencies of Thomas Jefferson and James Madison was led by a company of able preachers, including Francis Asbury, who were certain that the promotion of entire sanctification was the way to Christianize the nation. Contrary to what my reading of other historians of Methodism once inclined me to believe, the preaching of perfect love did thrive on the wilderness frontiers of northwestern Ohio and western Kentucky.

> THEY EACH THOUGHT THE DOCTRINE OF PERFECT LOVE WAS THE JEWEL OF METHODIST RELIGION.

It also flourished in the villages and small towns of New York's Hudson Valley. Here Freeborn Garretson found his wife and displayed the persuasive eloquence that made him Asbury's right-hand man for the rest of his days. In a brief memoir of her husband, Mrs. Garretson said she wanted Methodists to remember that "he lived and died a witness of that doctrine he delighted to preach, perfect love." In this he resembled the others who led the advance in the urban East—Ezekiel Cooper, Jesse Lee, Joshua Soule, George Pickering, Nathan Bangs, and Elijah Hedding. Their journals, biographies, and sermons testify that, despite occasional differences on other matters, they each thought the doctrine of perfect love was the jewel of Methodist religion. And they set that gem, as Wesley and Fletcher had, at the center of the story of redemption that gave unity to the Hebrew and Christian Scriptures.

When, around 1818, a resurgence of the teaching and experience of sanctification became evident in Boston, New York, and Baltimore, no Methodist questioned its consistency with what had gone before, either in urban or frontier America or in the British Methodism of Wesley's last decade. Moreover, the sequence of events in these early years of the North American Holiness crusade demonstrates how closely the Methodist network held city and countryside together. In 1818 a presiding elder reported that in widespread revivals in the Oneida, New York, District, many were "seeking for pardon" and others "breathing for perfect love." Soon after, a group of laypersons in New York City led their class and prayer meetings in seeking purity of heart, prompting the publication of inexpensive editions of Wesley's *Plain Account* and Fletcher's *Address to Imperfect Christians*.

Reports of upstate revivals and camp meetings that appeared in the New

York *Christian Advocate* in 1826, its first year of publication, described believers crying earnestly "for clean hearts," for "the treasure of holiness," and for "all the fullness of God." From Ithaca, New York, the presiding elder wrote of a traveling minister who joined scores of others in seeking to be "fully renewed in the image of God" after a sermon based on Paul's question addressed to the Ephesian congregation, "Have ye received the Holy Ghost since ye believed?" (Acts 19:2).

Reporters of New England camp meetings routinely listed the numbers of unbelievers converted, backsliders reclaimed, and believers who were seeking or who had found entire sanctification. Late in 1823 a pastor recently stationed at Eastham, Massachusetts, on Cape Cod, wrote the editors of *Zion's Herald* that during the fall a women's prayer meeting had prompted the people to "press forward" toward their "high calling." Many of them, he wrote, "have been baptized with the Holy Ghost, and do testify boldly that perfect love casteth out every slavish fear."

In 1824 the Methodist book agents published Timothy Merritt's *The Christian's Manual: A Treatise on Christian Perfection, with Directions for Obtaining That State.* Writing principally for Methodist readers, he laced the book with long quotations from Wesley's key writings on the subject, in a manner that remained conventional throughout the rest of the century. Nine editions had appeared by 1840.

Merritt was an abolitionist in the 1830s and a friend of Orange Scott and others who during the next decade organized the Wesleyan Methodist secession and provoked the division of the parent denomination into North and South. In 1839 Merritt became the founding editor of the Boston monthly *Guide to Christian Perfection,* soon renamed *Guide to Holiness.* For 60 years it was the organ of the American Holiness Movement.

The relationship of the emphasis on entire sanctification to the spiritual leadership of women was likewise rooted in English Methodism, where Hester Ann Rogers and Mary Bossanquet, John Fletcher's wife, set the pace. At the beginning of 1824, *Zion's Herald* adorned its new "Ladies' Department" with a brief biography of Mrs. Fletcher, emphasizing her spiritual leadership of her husband's Anglican parish after his death. Two sisters, Sarah Lankford and Phoebe Palmer, both born in England, were members of Nathan Bangs' class meeting in New York during the 1820s. They sought and believed they experienced purity of heart. In 1836 they began the famous New York Tuesday Meeting for the Promotion of Holiness. During the next 40 years, they led hundreds of Methodist ministers' wives and their husbands into the same experience.

Another symbol of the power of this American Wesleyan culture appears in the sermon that Peter Jones, a converted Indian chief, preached on the text "Blessed are the pure in heart" in his famous visit to London in January 1832. Jones no doubt preached what he had heard for years from Methodist missionaries to the Wyandots. "It is possible for us sinful creatures to be made pure in heart" by the power of the "Great Spirit," he declared—to be "saved from our sins" and "washed in the blood of Christ, and . . . cleansed from all unrighteousness."

It would be quite out of order to bring this introductory chapter on the transference of Wesley's movement from England to America to the sort of conclusion we historians love. We commonly look for signs of incipient decline to allow us the occasion to look backward in summary and interpretation. But the essence of much of this volume is continuity. When one adds to all the cultural dynamics inherent in such movements the conviction that the Maker of heaven and earth is present in their midst—granting each member deliverance from the guilt and power of what he or she had believed was evil, bringing "righteousness, peace, and joy," and assuring each one an eternal life of holiness and happiness—when this assurance is present, the power of a popular religious movement to perpetuate itself is indeed formidable.

Originally published as chapter 1 in *Great Holiness Classics, Vol. 4: The 19th-Century Holiness Movement* (Kansas City: Beacon Hill Press of Kansas City, 1998), 31-39.

We dare not fight
intramural theological battles
at a time of widespread
search for spirituality
among the general public
and a specific desire
for personal wholeness
among believers.

—David L. McKenna

From *Wesleyan Leadership in Troubled Times* (Kansas City: Beacon Hill Press of Kansas City, 2002), 75.

# 4

# HOLINESS: HEART OF CHRISTIAN LIVING
## —Holiness as Doctrine, Experience, and Life—

## J. B. Chapman

PERHAPS IT IS SOMETHING of a play on words, but usually we speak of a thing as attained when it is reached as a result of human endeavor, and we speak of a thing as being obtained when it comes as the gift of another upon terms that decidedly favor the receiver. And we think it is not an accident that the word "receive" is used in such passages as Acts 26:18, "That they might receive forgiveness of sins and inheritance among them which are sanctified by faith that is in me." Holiness is not an accomplishment, but is a gift received. It is not attained, but is obtained from the Lord. It is not to be approximated by endeavor, but is to be accomplished by the divine enablement. It is wrought as an instantaneous crisis, and not possessed by means of a gradual approach.

### HOLINESS: A DOCTRINE TO BELIEVE

*(1) The first step toward obtaining this blessing is to see and acknowledge its desirability.* The commands and promises of the Word of God should help us in this. Knowing our God is infinite in goodness, we can but know that that which He commands is for our highest good, and that which He so frequently and forcibly promises He is able to perform. Then we have all had sufficient contact with saintly souls to cause us to see the possibility and desirability of being free from sin and holy in heart. It is beside the question for us to recall that there are those who claim it who do not live it. There are some who claim it who do live it, and most of us have seen such undeniable demonstrations of the truth of this blessed word. Then we have, practically all of us, found ourselves face to face with tasks for which we were spiritually unprepared. This is a challenge to us to go earnestly after the promised blessing that will make us ready to do every good work.

43

*(2) The second step toward obtaining the blessing is to choose definitely to have it.* By every means God appeals to us, but He by no means compels us. Desire alone is not sufficient. Desire alone may easily degenerate into a weak wish. Choice is a human faculty, and stands for stamina and determination. It is represented by "I will." It first counts the cost and then discounts it in favor of the prize to be won.

> **REPENTANCE HAS TO DO WITH THAT WHICH IS WRONG; CONSECRATION HAS TO DO WITH THAT WHICH IS RIGHT.**

*(3) The third step toward obtaining the blessing is consecration.* Consecration differs from repentance in this: repentance has to do with that which is wrong; consecration has to do with that which is right. Repentance is forsaking evil; consecration is presenting that which is good to God. A sinner cannot consecrate until he repents and finds pardon, for consecration is the devotion of the life and talents—not the abandoning of transgression. We mentioned once before that this is a condition that must be met before one can be sanctified, and yet it is a condition that cannot be met until after we are justified, therefore this alone would establish the doctrine that we are sanctified after we are justified and that sanctification is properly called the second blessing. To be valid as a condition for this blessing, consecration must be complete—without hesitation and without reservation. It must be a devotement to God, and not to just some particular work to which one may find himself drawn. The prayer is:

> *Take my life and let it be, consecrated, Lord, to Thee . . .*
> *Take myself and I shall be, ever, only, all for Thee.*

*(4) The fourth step toward obtaining the blessing is faith.* Faith for this particular thing. Here you have come as a justified Christian, assured by the inner witness of the Holy Spirit that you are a child of God. You have found by reading the Bible and searching your own heart that God commands you to be holy and that He has provided the means for making you so. You have desired this blessing and chosen it with its cost before you. You have now brought your all to the altar of God in consecration. You have dedicated yourself and all you are and all you ever expect to be to God to be used of Him in any way that He sees best. So far as you are able to do it, you have sanctified yourself by complete consecration. You have asked God to sanctify you by complete purification. He has promised to do it. You have brought yourself to Him in the fullest condition. You believe He is willing and able to make you holy, and that He is ready to do it this very hour. There is nothing more that God can do in promising. There is nothing more that you can do in meeting the conditions of His promises. To hesitate is to doubt and indicate your uncertainty as to whether He will do what He has said. So without fear and without hesitation, you step right out on the promise and announce to three worlds, "I believe that Jesus Christ sanctifies me now."

The steps have been taken. They are like the steps to Solomon's ivory throne. The only one left is the top of the throne itself—the blessing that God has promised.

Will it fail? Will He fail? To ask is to answer. He will not fail. He will come in sanctifying fullness and make your heart His throne. He will purge out the dross of inbred sin and make you clean. He will fill and possess and rule and make you "all glorious within." It will henceforth be your delight to tell among men and angels what wonderful things He has wrought for you and in your heart. You have found your Beulah Land, your Canaan, your inheritance that shall never fail. Henceforth you shall walk in the way of holiness where neither lion nor ravenous beast is found. I join you in praise. I sing hallelujah, "The Comforter has come!"

## HOLINESS: AN EXPERIENCE TO RECEIVE

In John 17:17 we are told that we are sanctified through the truth, and further we are told, "Thy word is truth." We understand, then, that the Master was describing the place of the Bible as the Word of God in its relation to the blessing of entire sanctification by means of which we are made holy. In Acts 26:18 we are said to be sanctified by faith. In Heb. 13:12 we are told that we are sanctified by the blood. In Rom. 15:16 we are described as sanctified by the Holy Ghost. But we all know the Bible, the blood of Jesus, faith, and the Holy Spirit are not interchangeable words, and we know also that we cannot be allowed to choose alternate ways of being sanctified. We never expect to find one Christian sanctified by the Bible, another by the blood, another by faith, and another by the Holy Ghost. It must be that whoever is sanctified at all must be sanctified by all the means mentioned. What then is the explanation?

The theologians tell us we are to be sanctified *instrumentally* by the Word of God, *efficaciously* by the blood of Jesus, *conditionally* by faith, and *efficiently* by the Holy Ghost. By this we understand that the Bible is our infallible guide as to the manner we are to go about it to seek and find this blessing. The blood of Jesus is the meritorious price paid for its purchase. Faith is the one prime condition we must meet. And the Holy Spirit is the actual agent for changing, purging, and filling our hearts. Only Spirit can change spirit, and that is why we cannot ascribe the efficient agency to anyone or anything except the Holy Spirit who was very properly designated by Dr. Daniel Steele as "The Executor of God in the work of salvation."

**THE OPINIONS OF OTHERS WILL NOT SUFFICE.**

In a matter so important as our state and standing with God we need a sure word. The opinions of others will not suffice. Creeds and statements wrought out in councils are valuable only when they are true interpretations of the divine Word. But God has given us an inspired and infallible Bible. Whosoever speaks contrary to this Word is to be rejected. The Bible is the touchstone of all doctrine. It is the dependable revelation of the will of God and the way to God. If we get sanctified at all we must get it according to the terms laid down in the Word. Bible holiness is the only true holiness.

There is no merit in works or words or tears or anything else we can bring. The blood of Jesus alone is the price of our redemption. When we come to be cleansed from all sin we have no plea but the blood. No matter how many years we have served God, we have done only that which it was our duty to do. No matter how much we have given of time or money for the advancement of His kingdom, we have given nothing that we did not first receive. The blood of Jesus alone has merit, and by it alone we have entrance into the holy of holies— the divine presence—where we find the cleansing we crave.

Faith has its prerequisites, as repentance in asking for pardon, consecration in asking for holiness, and obedience in praying for persevering grace. But faith remains the one and only prime condition. Faith is the one thing without which there is no deliverance, and when it is present there is always deliverance. Prerequisites lead to faith and faith leads to victory. Faith is not a force within itself but is the means by which the power of God is released upon us. Faith salvation, like faith healing, is a purely human thing. Faith is just the condition. God is the power.

## THE HOLY SPIRIT IS A PERSON.

The Holy Spirit is a person, but He has different offices. The Holy Spirit comes in convicting office to the sinner. He comes in regenerating office to the penitent believer. He comes in sanctifying office to the consecrating, accepting believer. There is no reason for confusion regarding whether the Holy Spirit comes in regeneration or only in entire sanctification. He comes in both instances. But in the latter instance He comes in fullness and power. On the Day of Pentecost He came in tongues of fire, as well as in the likeness of a rushing mighty wind. Fire is the emblem of purifying. There are many symbols of the Holy Spirit and His works in the Bible.

In His life-giving power He is like the wind, as Jesus told Nicodemus in John 3.

In His regenerating office He is like water (Titus 3:5).

In His feeding office He is like milk (Isa. 55).

In His purifying and energizing power He is like fire. The deeper purging represented by fire in contrast with the more outward cleansing effects of water is well known in the realm of natural things, and the Spirit uses this common knowledge to make clear the distinction between the work of regeneration— a washing—and entire sanctification—a purging with fire.

How fully then is the way to holiness set before us. We come as we are taught in the Bible. We bring the blood of Jesus as our merit. We exercise faith as the condition. The Holy Spirit answers to the blood by coming as the vital agency of our full purifying.

I once likened the four factors here considered to getting goods from a mail order house. There is the catalog that describes the goods, states the price, and gives directions for ordering. This is analogous to the place of the Bible in our sanctification. There is the money required which is in the position of the blood in our sanctification. There is the act of sending forth the order by mail—an act that passes beyond sight, and is analogous to faith. Then there are the goods actually delivered to the door by the postman, and this is like the coming of the Holy Spirit in Pentecostal fullness. Surely none of us should go farther without the blessing. The Word is true and dependable. The blood has all merit. Faith has every ground. The Holy Spirit waits at the door. Today, even this hour, "Wilt thou be made whole?"

## HOLINESS: A LIFE TO BE LIVED

Holiness is a doctrine to be believed, an experience to be received, and a life to be lived. As a doctrine it is the central thesis of the Bible. As an experience it is the heart of all the verities in the dealing of human beings with God in the things of the soul. As a life to be lived it is from every point of view the best life possible.

**IT IS FROM EVERY POINT OF VIEW THE BEST LIFE POSSIBLE.**

There are two contrasting evils, toward one or the other of which we all tend to a greater or lesser extent: one is to lower the standard to the point where we can reach it without the grace God proposes to give us, and the other is to hold up a standard impossible even to the best of people. And strangely enough, the practical results are about the same in both cases.

The standard should remain where God puts it. At such a point we shall need all that grace can do for us to enable us to reach it, and yet by the grace of God we shall be able to reach it with joy and gladness. On the principle that the righteous are scarcely saved, and yet they are abundantly saved, when we fail by refusing the grace of God we fail miserably, and when we succeed by obtaining His grace we succeed gloriously. There is, indeed, a twilight zone between outbroken sin and the fullness of grace, where the appeal of the world is still strong and yet the call of God is more or less effective. But that zone should be crossed, not made a place of permanent dwelling.

Division of a subject sometimes helps us in grasping it, so let us think of conduct in three parts: in our relationship to ourselves, in our relationship to others of humankind, and in our relationship to God. Then we shall have a summary in Titus 2:11-12, where it is said the grace of God teaches us to deny ungodliness and worldly lusts, and that we should live "soberly, righteously, and godly, in this present world." To *deny* ungodliness and worldly lusts means to turn away from them, to forsake them, to refuse to indulge in them. *Ungodliness* is a word describing wicked conduct and *worldly lusts* a term describing unholy thinking and desires. To deny these is to become outwardly and inwardly good in the negative sense. It involves harmlessness. It describes the passive virtues.

But holiness is more than negative goodness. It is positive goodness also. Taken apart, the statement is that we are to live soberly *toward* ourselves, righteously toward our neighbors, and godly toward our Heavenly Father.

## In Relationship to Self

*Sobriety* is just another word for temperance. *Temperance,* in turn, is defined as *self-control.* To live by this rule is to refuse tangents. To govern the temper and the will. To think soundly. To speak gently. To eat and sleep and work with neither sloth nor excess. To check the inner conscience sincerely. To face one's limitations faithfully. To speak the truth in word and in heart. To speak no ill of his neighbor. To neither minimize nor exaggerate. To be transparent before the bar of God and one's own moral judgment. To testify faithfully. And to pray unpretentiously.

## In Relationship to Others

To live righteously toward our neighbor is to be clean in our social relations. To be honest in our business relations. To be truthful in our communications. To be fair in our judgment of the deeds, words, and motives of others. The righteous person is a faithful friend, a good spouse, child and sibling, an agreeable neighbor, a helper of the needy, a forgiver of enemies, an upright citizen, a supporter of civic well-being, a careful taxpayer, an observer of law and order, and a doer of good deeds.

## In Relationship to God

To live godly is to live in the fear and love of God. To be obedient to all His known will. To worship God *only,* according to the First Commandment; to worship Him *spiritually,* according to the Second Commandment; to worship Him *reverently,* according to the Third Commandment; to worship Him *statedly*, according to the Fourth Commandment. It is to worship with the hand by tithing the income and making gifts according to the ability that God gives. It is to worship with the mind by reading God's Word and meditating upon His power, wisdom, and love. It is to worship Him with the heart by pouring out the heart in prayer, praise, and giving of thanks. It is to live always in the attitude of willingness to give up what you seem to possess and to receive whatever He may choose to give. To live godly is to live in gracious communion, fellowship, and agreement with God.

If any are struck with the thought that we cannot live godly, because we are but finite and God is infinite, then let them remember that it is quality and likeness and not quantity and identity that are required. We can be like God in the sense that a drop of ocean water is like the ocean.

A visitor to a clock and watch exhibition saw there a clock so large that the dial was fifty-two feet across and the minute hand was twenty-six feet in length. Then there were smaller clocks ranging on down to wall clocks, mantel clocks, and table alarm clocks. Then there were large, heavy watches, smaller gentlemen's watches, large-sized ladies' watches, wrist watches, and on down to one with a dial so tiny that one could not see the position of the hands except by use of a magnifying glass. But all the clocks and watches, great and small, were good timekeepers, and were kept regulated and set by experts, so that they were in perfect agreement. When the big clock up at the head of the line said, "Twelve o'clock" and the clocks and watches along the line said, "twelve o'clock," the little tiny one at the very foot spoke up in unison with the others and said, "twelve o'clock." The little watch was not the big clock, but it was in perfect accord with it.

And it is in something of that sense that we can be godly "in this present world." For our present purpose it is superfluous to add those final words, for it is in this sense only that we can be godly even in heaven. And it is to the glory of His grace that God can so save and keep us that we can live truly godly right here where Satan is loosed and temptation is rife—and that we can live so all the days of our lives (Luke 1:73-75).

Originally published as chapters 6 through 8 of *Holiness: The Heart of Christian Experience* (Kansas City: Nazarene Publishing House, 1943), 28-40.

The gift purifies

the heart.

That means the destruction

of the body of sin,

the removal of the carnal mind.

It is more than

a housecleaning.

This gift is the gift

of himself.

The house is cleansed,

purified, in order to receive

the Guest.

—Phineas F. Bresee

From *The Quotable Bresee,* Harold Ivan Smith, comp. (Kansas City: Beacon Hill Press of Kansas City, 1983), 54.

# 5

# IN SEARCH FOR THE CAUSE OF SPIRITUAL FAILURE
## —The Rebel Within—

## Richard S. Taylor

SCRIPTURES FOR BACKGROUND: Jer. 17:9-10; Mark 7:14-23; Acts 5:1-11; Rom. 7:7—8:39; James 4:1-10 (RSV)

It is always possible to pin the blame for the Christian's failure on something which happened, or on some blundering person who got in the way just at the wrong time. Too often this is exactly what the defeated Christian does. He rationalizes and consequently is full of tricks. He always has an explanation for his bitterness, or sharp tongue, or his twists and turns. But the more he hides behind his alibis, the more confused becomes his spiritual life.

Sometimes even religious teachers can produce ego-salving props for the misbehaving Christian. "After all, the Corinthians had just recently been saved out of raw, barbarous paganism. You couldn't expect them to do any better!" *But Paul did.* Or, "You must take into consideration his background! He was spoiled, you know. Give him time and he will get over his selfishness." But some have been "getting over it" for many years now, with little visible improvement.

Such leaders would be wiser to try to help under-par Christians stop looking at people and circumstances, and begin looking within. For that is what they must do in soul-wrenching honesty and humility.

## SOME PLAUSIBLE ALIBIS

But even when we look "within" it is possible to come up with the wrong diagnosis. For example, the Christian's failure may be ascribed to (1) immaturity, (2) temperament, or (3) physical condition.

### 1. Is the problem of a Christian's failing simply a matter of newness?

If so, more practice and experience in the Christian way will remedy it. Is it ignorance only—ignorance of the Bible and Satan and the world? Then in that case intense application to study will remedy his deficiency and in so doing will sweeten his disposition.

## 2. Is the problem basically a matter of natural temperament that time and maturity will discipline? Is wrong training the culprit?

This often is offered as an explanation for the spitefulness and self-assertion and insubordination of the out-of-joint Christian. Or are some believers constantly full of doubts and uncertainties and arguments and objections simply because they are *superior thinkers*? If such is the cause, then to become a saint the super-intellectual either should stop thinking or find all the answers. The achievement of sainthood would thus depend on acquiring large amounts of training and knowledge.

But anyone who knows human nature and has studied Christians is painfully aware that these are not the paths to sainthood. The trained, skillful, experienced, knowledgeable, and positionally "secure" Christians can be as proud, self-seeking, unloving, and carnally cantankerous as anyone. If holiness and Christlikeness are only a matter of natural disposition, then many Christians will never be Christlike, for they were not fortunate enough to be born with the right disposition. In that case the great commandments will seem unfair to them.

## 3. There is yet another possible explanation for the Christian's failure: physical condition.

The wear and tear of life, the strain on one's nervous system, the usual tensions and anxieties bring one to breakdowns, impatience, and unkindness. All human beings have their limit, it is often said; they can "take" only so much. When that time comes something snaps, and usually it is their religion. It may be in the form of a blowup or in the form of collapse of confidence. Weariness makes depression easy; depression makes doubt easy; doubt leads to darkness. The whole problem seen in this light is caused by our being so utterly human. One day a Christian may be a shining saint, with Christlikeness and love exuding from him. But this is because he *feels* good; he had a good night's rest; and his liver is in good order. The next week physical sluggishness may change his mood completely and in his headachy, nervous jumpiness he will scream at the children.

OLD-FASHIONED PEOPLE KEPT PRAYING ABOUT THESE CHANGES IN MOODS AND ERUPTIONS OF UGLINESS UNTIL GOD EITHER DELIVERED THEM OR GAVE THE GRACE FOR SELF-DISCIPLINE.

Old-fashioned people kept praying about these changes in moods and eruptions of ugliness until God either delivered them or gave the grace for self-discipline. These days we have gotten "wise"; we take a pill. Or at least we have a physical explanation for all our reactions. But let us beware lest we surrender our souls to the behaviorists and the materialists. If this is the full explanation, then our "saintliness" is purely a psychosomatic phenomenon, and our "Christlikeness" is merely mental health. Good religion becomes more dependent upon the right doctor than upon the right creed. But in this case also the soul is epiphenomenal—we are but blobs of animated matter in a deterministic universe, and the idea of "grace" is an illusion.

But the Christian knows better than this. He knows that somewhere entangled with his upset liver, jangled nerves, and weariness and headache, is a responsible moral agent whom God expects to keep right on trusting and loving in spite of it all, and who is keenly aware of sin when he doesn't. The godless psychiatrist may advise, "Blow your top!" "It will be good for you to get it off your chest!" But the puzzled Christian does not feel that his explosion has been "good" for him or anyone else. In his heart of hearts he cannot escape the conviction that surely there is a better way.

But we must back up now to concede that our physical state and the wear and tear of life do have a lot to do with our feelings. Because of this, it is true, we do need to learn to *live*—to negotiate life as wise men and women. We need to get the proper rest, learn when to stop, learn how to relax, learn how to pray and meditate, to feed on the Scriptures, to eat sensibly, and above all, learn to understand and discipline our moods.

But is this the total problem?

If the Christian's failure can be explained solely in terms of his haphazardness and his failure to understand himself and his moods, then of course it is obvious that the cure for his failure is simply growth in grace, with generous amounts of discipline. Efficiency, quietness, and poise, irradiated by love with all of its prismatic colors, will gradually emerge out of the learning process. All we need to do is give ourselves a little time. The hectic and lawless elements of our souls will disappear when once we get our work and time well organized and regulated. If we have been tied up inwardly with resentments and fears and bitterness, they will dissolve with improved poise and mature understanding. This, of course, is what we would call the achievement of saintliness by growth. This is entirely reasonable on the supposition that the regenerated Christian is basically sound with nothing *fundamentally* wrong with him. But this is precisely the problem. A house occupied by the right owner and built on the right site, and *basically* sound, may need only a little paint. But if the timbers are weak and termites are boring, that is something else.

The Christian "temple" belongs to the right owner, and is built on the right site, but is it thoroughly *sound*? What is the cause of the Christian's failure?

## THE BIBLE ANSWER

Christians will prefer face-saving explanations, and to begin with often will try to solve their problems on the basis of them. So they will study, pray, throw themselves zealously into the Lord's work, and accelerate spiritual activity in general, trying to elude the wobble in the wheel. But if they take God's promises and commands seriously and if they take their failure seriously, they will sooner or later be tempted to despair. As they come to see that increased knowledge and skill have not cleansed them from their inner sinful attitudes, or cured their selfish traits, they may become disillusioned. But at this point they will begin to see that, while the *occasions* that stimulate these sinful attitudes and selfish traits may be many and varied, these occasions are not the *cause*. The cause lies farther back, deep in the self-nature. If the Christian gets wise to himself to this extent, he will begin to doubt the magic efficacy of time, growth, and discipline as his sanctifiers. He may suspect a crookedness in the axle of the soul that mere acceleration will not straighten out.

At this stage he may have some measure of sympathetic understanding of Oswald Chambers, who reached the same place after four years of Christian living. He came to the desperate conclusion that if what he had "was all the Christianity there was, the thing was a fraud."[1] This is a little reminiscent of the anguished cry in Rom. 7:24: "O wretched man that I am! who shall deliver me from the body of this death?"

No, sound holiness and perfect love come as gifts of divine grace through the Holy Spirit, and not as achievements dependent on either time, growth, or purely human advantages. Yet it is obvious that sufficient grace is not experienced in conversion or the new birth. What is the impediment?

The Bible teaches that the real underlying cause of chronic failure in the Christian life is *an inherited evil bias in one's moral nature, not remedied by regeneration.*

**An evil heart.** Jeremiah paints a dismal picture of the human heart. He says it is "deceitful above all things, and desperately wicked: who can know it?" (17:9). Jesus does not relieve the picture at all. He says: "For from within, out of the heart of men, proceed evil thoughts, adulteries, fornications, murders, thefts, covetousness . . . pride, foolishness" (Mark 7:21-22). Yet some of these evidences of evil cropped out in both the disciples and the Corinthians. This would prove that, no matter how radically changed they were in heart, they were not entirely changed. This makes all the more significant the adjective *pure,* in Matt. 5:8 and 1 Tim. 1:5. It is even more significant in Acts 15:9, when the full cleansing of the heart is tied in with the baptism with the Holy Spirit. It is clear that a principle of evil still lurks in a heart that may be regenerated, yet not filled with the Holy Spirit. There is a backsliding tendency in the heart.

**The carnal mind.** In Rom. 8:5-7, Paul speaks of the carnal mind, by which he means, not the intellect, but the disposition, tendency, or inclination of the soul. The carnal mind is the disposition to seek the fleshly pattern of living. It is that nature which is perversely responsive to sin. It is downward, earthly, and physical in its tendencies.

The unholiness of the carnal mind is seen in its essential and spontaneous antagonism to God; it "is enmity against God: for it is not subject to the law of God, neither indeed can be" (v. 7). Dr. Samuel Young speaks of this mind as "the principle that wars against the will of God." Again he defines it as "the loadstone to evil."

Quite obviously this is not a specific evil action but the selfish bias *behind* the evil action. In this sense it is what a man *is* more than what he does. One is the root, the other the fruit.

THIS IS NOT A SPECIFIC EVIL ACTION BUT THE SELFISH BIAS *BEHIND* THE EVIL ACTION.

*The law of sin.* Paul also calls this evil propensity "the law of sin." This discussion is in Rom. 7:7—8:4. Here, too, Paul talks about sin, not as a series of individual acts, but as a *bent to sin* that prompts the acts. This bent is not an occasional quirk, but the universal trait of the human race, and a constant moral quality in every individual of the race. This is why Paul calls it the "sin that dwelleth in me." It is not a "law" in the sense of a statute that has been passed, but a law like gravitation. This means that a man *finds it* within himself; he does not create it. It means further that its operation is uniform and predictable—always in the same direction. "For I delight in the law of God after the inward man: But I see another law in my members, warring against the law of my mind, and bringing me into captivity to the law of sin which is in my members" (7:22-23).

The law of sin is truly a "body of death," for it demands ultimate and final separation from God. The same thing is said of the carnal mind, which is obviously the law of sin under a different name: "To be carnally minded is death." Unless therefore there is a way to be rid of the carnal mind, the infected believer still has the sentence of death *within*, even though personal sins have been pardoned. Truly the soul needs a *double* cure—not only pardon, but purity.

This then is the substratum of sinfulness in human nature by which all men are sinners. Paul explains it this way: "But I am carnal, sold under sin" (7:14). Apart from his own volition, he was already delivered to the power of sin. Who sold him? Adam. With all other descendants of Adam, Paul shared a common bondage. The sin nature, he makes clear, was in him from birth. It did not begin in him when he committed his first sin; it was prior to it as its prompter (7:9-11).

We are reaching now the crux of the matter, and the answer to the problem of the Christian's failure. For while justification by faith deals with a human's personal guilt (those sins that he has willingly committed) and purges him from the accumulated depravity resulting from those sins, it does not cleanse his nature from the moral twist he *inherited*. Conversion makes a person become again as a "little child" (Matt. 18:3) in his simplicity of heart and cleanness before God; but it does not take him beyond the state of the child, which is a carnal state.

Let us put it yet another way. Regeneration imparts a new nature, inclined toward spiritual things, without totally removing the old nature. Hence it is possible for the Bible to speak of the "double minded" (James 1:8; 4:8).[2] This can, of course, be interpreted as the vacillation of one who wavers because he can't quite make up his mind; and in this sense, the Christian finds himself fluctuating between two opinions. But the meaning is deeper than this. He is swinging between two *dispositions,* so that there is an inward conflict. Sometimes the carnal mind seems stronger, and at other times the new mind is stronger. But meanwhile he cannot do the things that he would.

Two patterns of living, two sets of values, as the twins struggling within Rebekah, are contesting within the Christian for absolute loyalty and complete mastery. It was this dual state that made the disciples such inconsistent and unpredictable followers of Jesus. This is why Jesus could acknowledge them as true disciples, yet pronounce them "evil" (Luke 11:13). This also explains why Paul could call the Corinthians "yet carnal." Both the disciples and the Corinthians were spiritually alive but they were not yet entirely holy in heart. This lurking carnal nature imparted an element of evil to their character, in spite of their good intentions and their love for Jesus. "This inner disease broke out" (like measles) in their "envying, and strife, and divisions."[3]

## THE REBEL WITHIN

There is an interesting construction in the Greek of Paul's testimony to the Galatians: "I have been crucified with Christ: it is no longer I who live, but Christ who lives in me; and the life I now live in the flesh I live by faith in the Son of God" (2:20, RSV). Notice the many first-person pronouns used. But in the Greek the word for I (*ego*) is used only once—and that is the "I" that is slain on the Cross! Every other "I" is hidden in a verb, completely out of sight! Phillips brings out this remarkable distinction this way: "And my present life is not that of the old 'I' but the living Christ within me."

Sometimes, it is true, we use the term "ego" as a synonym for the self, and that, as a metaphysical entity, is indestructible. Without the ego, in this sense, we would be nonexistent as persons. But Paul in this verse *seems* to be giving the word a spiritual connotation; he associates it with an evil, past self, which has been put away. He is still a person—still a metaphysical self—so can still refer to himself. But the *ego,* as constituting an independent self-centeredness, a hard core of self-idolatry, in other words, the "BIG I," is gone. Immediately we think of some rather uncomplimentary modern variations: *egoism,* which the dictionary defines as excessive self-interest and *egotism,* which we quickly recognize as a synonym for conceit.

This "BIG I" is seen to be nothing other than the "law of sin," the "carnal mind," and the "evil heart of unbelief," with the mask off. It is the disposition to relate everything to self and its interests, to a selfish and rebellious degree. The very essence of this indwelling sin therefore is a fundamental bent toward self-authority or self-sovereignty. John calls it "lawlessness" (1 John 3:4, RSV). As we have noted before, Paul says, "It is not subject to the law of God, neither indeed can be" (Rom. 8:7). For in its very nature it is rebellion. Paul Updike says: "The spirit of independency is of the essence of carnality." Its sinfulness lies in the fact that whether intended or not, or fully realized or not, this independency is toward God as well as toward men. A spirit of independency toward men might in some circumstances be necessary, but a resistance to God's yoke is sinful.

> PRIDE EXALTS SELF AS THE SUPREME VALUE.

Pride and unbelief are inseparable aspects of this inner core of self-willfulness and self-love. Pride exalts self as the supreme value, while unbelief exalts self as the supreme authority. Men do not believe God because they would rather believe themselves.

Let us see how this self-exaltation lines up with Rom. 12:1-2. William L. Bradley says: "The Cross is not only an event in history, though certainly it is not less than this, but it is repeated in climactic fashion in every human situation when men come face to face with the ultimate problem of Self." This, he goes on to say, arouses a "deadly inner conflict," which man naturally tries to evade by retreating to the safety of abstract truth and academic discussions. "It is not easy," he says, "to be faced with questions of ultimate concern when they confront us with the fact of an inevitable death which will wrench us from the treasures we have industriously collected for ourselves." The real struggle is in giving up what Oswald Chambers calls "our right to ourselves." Bradley expresses it vividly:

> What assurance have we that there will be anything left of us if we sacrifice every shred of self-hood, of self-respect, of the "I" which at least we can claim as our very own? No one can take our last bit of pride from us, and here is Christ demanding that we give it up to God right now.

What is the spontaneous reaction of the carnal self to this radical demand? "Naturally we strike back at Him," is the way Bradley puts it. "Quite normally we reject Him at this point."[4]

This irrational struggle of the Christian who has once said, "Yes," with a remaining inward "No" can be seen in the concrete reactions of some representative persons.

Fred Dalzell, a converted Communist, testifies in the *Flame* that after he was saved he became aware of his spiritual lack, and of an increasing hunger for the fullness of the Holy Spirit. In a service one day, he says, "The challenge was made to seek full salvation; but my heart remained stubborn."

David Ramirez, a Harvard Ph.D. who became the founder of Nazarene missions in his native Nicaragua, heard H. V. Miller preach on holiness in Chicago. Though he had been converted as a youth, and had recently been reclaimed after many years of wandering, this was his first exposure to the doctrine of entire sanctification. His trained mind, a doctorate both in philosophy and psychology, instantly grasped the radical implications of what Dr. Miller was saying. He reacted violently. On the way home he protested to his friend that Dr. Miller was wrong; that no one should so completely surrender himself, not even to God! A week of Bible study attempting to disprove the preacher resulted in intense conviction instead, and the next Sunday found him at the public altar making the very absolute surrender which his carnal heart had so violently protested.[5]

This state in which there are both a "yes" and a "no" struggling for final supremacy in the heart will not be a permanent state. There will be a victor. If the "no" is final victor, then Christ and the Christian are defeated. For, to quote again from William L. Bradley: "In asserting the autonomy of our wills we destroy the possibility of our spiritual freedom. We reject—we disclaim—what we know to be our true destiny." Therefore no inquiry could be more crucial than this inquiry into the nature of the believer's failure—or rather the nature of its *cause.* Only then can we inquire concerning a cure. "The answer to the problem of true life," concludes Bradley, "thus lies at the center of the self and its ultimate loyalty."

---

1. Quoted by Paul Rees, *Stand Up in Praise to God* (Grand Rapids: Wm. B. Eerdmans Publishing Co., 1960), 91.

2. The Greek here is not the same as in Rom. 8:5-7. It is literally "two-souled." A. T. Robertson translates it: "double-souled, double-minded, Bunyan's 'Mr. Facing-both-way'" (*Word Pictures in the New Testament* [New York: Harper and Brothers Publishers, 1933]), VI, 15.

3. In view of this, the age-old debate about Rom. 7 (does it describe the carnal Christian or the awakened Jew under the law?) is a bit pointless. The chapter applies to whoever experiences the spiritual struggle described therein. And the Christian who has made an honest attempt to keep the carnal mind under, only to repeatedly fail, and who has finally seen the "groundwork of his heart" (John Wesley), will not hesitate to cry, "The picture is mine!" Of course he has a measure of victory over sin, just as did the disciples and the Corinthians, and in fact, as Paul did even before his conversion. But he will also be aware of a measure of bondage; and the more he craves holiness, the more anguished will be his or her cry, "O wretched man [person] that I am!"

The only way Rom. 7 can be restricted in its application to the unregenerate is to say that "indwelling sin," as an inherited principle of evil, is effectively dealt with in regeneration, so that the Christian no longer has a problem with it. If it is present it will become a problem—we can be sure of that—for it is "not subject to the law of God." But to assume that regeneration delivers from this bias to evil is to suppose an experience that neither the disciples (before Pentecost) nor the Corinthians enjoyed, and which never has been taught by any of the major orthodox creeds of Christendom. On the contrary, they have agreed that humans do come into the world with a sinful bias; that it does remain in the believer's heart, and that it does, though suppressed, become the Christian's supreme problem in the new life. And *this* is the real explanation for the Christian's failure.

Another technical but important problem has been whether or not Paul intended to teach that indwelling sin was an entity, or *real being.* That it is not a physical entity, as a rotten tooth, is surely obvious. Therefore when thinking of its eradication we must avoid the picture of an automobile accessory, such as a battery, which can be taken out, then replaced. Neither can it be said to be a metaphysical entity, strictly speaking, unless it is actually a form of demon possession, or psychic presence, as William Sanday seems to suggest. Even so, it is not a "thing in itself" that can exist apart from moral agents. *However,* we dare not tone down Paul's strong teaching here on the nature of this indwelling sin as a dynamic moral power in the soul that is subvolitional. Those who would explain away any positive concept of original sin have this chapter squared in their path. Toward a helpful solution might be two propositions:

*a.* It is essentially a deprivation, or lack, of the Holy Spirit. Richard Watson taught that man became depraved as a result of being deprived of the Holy Spirit. But while essentially negative, it is also positive, inasmuch as human personality is inherently dynamic; this being so, a person without God will be a dynamic *evil* person. Cold is nothing but the absence of heat; nevertheless a "cold wave" is a dynamic force, as anyone who has suffered its freezing power knows.

*b.* It can also be thought of as a dislocation, or disorganization, of instincts and faculties of the being, *around self rather than God.* Adam's choice of self rather than God resulted in an endemic self-orientation that thereafter prevailed in the race. This, of course, is the positive depravity that stemmed racially from Adam's deprivation.

Put these two ideas together and we see that man is cursed with a BIG "I" that will never be trimmed to size until completely recaptured, repossessed, and recontrolled by the Holy Spirit.

4. Excerpts from "The Authority of Jesus Christ," by William L. Bradley (professor of the philosophy of religion and chairman of the faculty of Hartford Theological Seminary), *Hartford Review,* 3rd quarter, 1961. Quoted by permission.

5. See *To Live Is Christ,* by Helen Temple (Kansas City: Beacon Hill Press, 1961). Ruth Paxson tells of a similar experience in her own Christian life in *Rivers of Living Water.*

Originally published as "In Search for the Cause," chapter 3 of *Life in the Spirit: Christian Holiness in Doctrine, Experience, and Life* (Kansas City: Nazarene Publishing House, 1966), 43-55.

The holiness which we find

everywhere emphasized

in the New Testament,

and exemplified in the life

of Jesus Christ,

is that state of spiritual life

where sin is shunned and hated;

where goodness is loved

for its own sake;

where the will is perfectly homed

in the will of God;

where the Holy Spirit dominates

the life in motive,

affection, and action.

—F. Watson Hannan

From "Jesus Cleanses the Temple" in *Great Holiness Classics, Vol. 5: Holiness Preachers and Preaching*, W. E. McCumber, ed. (Kansas City: Beacon Hill Press of Kansas City, 1989), 54.

# 6

# CRISIS AND PROCESS IN SANCTIFICATION
## —A DEFINING MOMENT STARTS A LIFE OF MEANING—

## W. T. Purkiser

THE QUESTION BEFORE US—does this experience of holiness result from growth and self-discipline, or is it an act of God's grace completed in a moment of time?

The concept of positional sanctification, the "Holy in Christ" view, is usually reinforced with two closely related assertions: that experimental sanctification is progressive and gradual and that it is completed only at or after death in the gathering of the saints in glory.

Let's begin with this quote from Lewis Sperry Chafer's *Systematic Theology.* After describing what he calls "positional sanctification," Chafer continues:

Second, experimental sanctification. This second aspect of the sanctifying work of God for the believer is progressive in some of its aspects, so is quite in contrast to the positional sanctification which is "once for all." It is accomplished by the power of God through the Spirit and through the Word: "Sanctify them through thy truth: thy word is truth" (John 17:17; see also 2 Corinthians 3:18; Ephesians 5:25-26; 1 Thessalonians 5:23; 2 Peter 3:18). Experimental sanctification is advanced according to various relationships. (1) In relation to the believer's yieldedness to God. In virtue of presenting his body a living sacrifice, the child of God thereby is set apart unto God and so is experimentally sanctified. The presentation may be absolute and thus admit of no progression, or it may be partial and so require a further development. In either case, it is a work of experimental sanctification. (2) In relation to sin. The child of God may so comply with every condition for true spirituality as to be experiencing all the provided deliverance and victory from the power of sin, or, on the other hand, he may be experiencing but a partial deliverance from the power of sin. In either case, he is set apart and thus is experimentally sanctified. (3) In relation to Christian growth. This aspect of experimental sanctification is progressive in every case. It therefore should in no way be confused with incomplete yieldedness to God or incomplete victory over sin. Its meaning is that the knowledge of truth, devotion, and Christian experience are naturally subject to development. In accord with their present state of development as Christians, believers experimentally are set apart unto God. And thus, again, the Christian is subject to an experimental sanctification which is progressive. . . . The Bible, therefore, does not teach that any child of God is altogether sanctified experimentally in daily life before that final consummation of all things.[1]

There is much in this quotation concerning growth in grace with which we should not quarrel. Our question concerns calling this "sanctification" and the assertion that experimental sanctification cannot therefore be completed. Other writers in similar vein add the idea that the sin nature may be progressively brought under control, mortified daily by careful attention to the means of grace, and that thereby the believer is being progressively sanctified by gaining greater and greater victory over sin in his life, and more and more control over the impulses of sin in his heart.

This puts the issue squarely before us. Entire sanctification, as understood by holiness people, does not admit of degrees. It is as perfect and complete in its kind as the work of regeneration and justification is perfect and complete in its kind. This does not mean that there is no growth in grace both before and after sanctification. What it does mean is that sanctification, as an act of God, is instantaneous and is not produced by growth or self-discipline or the progressive control of the carnal nature.

## SANCTIFICATION BY GROWTH

Before asking, "What saith the Lord?" let us give momentary consideration to the growth theory.

First, it is difficult to see in this anything more than a Blood-rejecting notion of sanctification by works and human striving. Pious words are uttered about the help of the Holy Spirit while the possibility of His dispensational work is denied. It is possible to give lip service to the Spirit's ministry and at the same time flatly to contradict His sanctifying Lordship.

Second, death is expected to complete what grace and the cross of Christ could not. Lurking back of all these speculations is the ghost of the ancient Gnostic heresy, that the physical body is in some sense the seat and source of sin. There is otherwise no logical reason for this persistent doubt that the redeemed soul may be free from sin here and now.

More crucial still is the fact that the Bible never intimates anywhere that either growth or death have the least thing to do with the soul's sanctification. Instead, the Word of God, the blood of Christ, the Holy Spirit, and faith are the factors indicated as concerned with sanctification. Growth is referred to as being *in* grace, never *into* grace. Growth always relates to increase in *quantity,* never to change in *quality.* Further, to suppose that physical death makes any change in the moral quality of the human soul is to go in direct opposition to the clear statements of the Word. "As the tree falls, so shall it lie."

## SANCTIFICATION AS A CRISIS EXPERIENCE

As we turn to the testimony of the Word, we find three classes of evidence that entire sanctification is, in fact, instantaneous and not gradual, a crisis experience and not an endless process. There is, first, the analogy to justification and the new birth. Second, there is the testimony of the terms used to describe the work—terms that customarily refer to actions completed at a given point in time. And, third, there is the logic of example found in the Bible. Let us look briefly at each.

**1. *The Analogy with the New Birth.*** Consider first the analogy found in the Bible between justification or the new birth, and sanctification or holiness. There are great points of similarity between these two works of divine grace.

Both justification and sanctification are products of divine love: John 3:16, "For God so loved the world that he gave his only begotten Son, that whosoever believeth in him should not perish, but have everlasting life," and Eph. 5:25-27, "Husbands, love your wives, even as Christ also loved the church, and gave himself for it; that he might sanctify and cleanse it with the washing of water by the word . . . that it should be holy and without blemish."

Both justification and sanctification are manifestations of God's good, acceptable, and perfect will: 1 Tim. 2:3-4, "For this is good and acceptable in the sight of God our Saviour: who will have all men to be saved, and to come unto the knowledge of the truth"; and Heb. 10:10, "By the which will [that is, the will of God as accomplished by Christ in his atoning death] we are sanctified through the offering of the body of Jesus Christ once for all."

> "SANCTIFY THEM THROUGH THY TRUTH: THY WORD IS TRUTH."

Both justification and sanctification are accomplished through the wonderful light of God's Word: 1 Pet. 1:23, "Being born again, not of corruptible seed, but of incorruptible, by the word of God, which liveth and abideth for ever"; and John 17:17, "Sanctify them through thy truth: thy word is truth."

Both justification and sanctification are wrought in the heart by the effective agency of the Holy Spirit of God: Titus 3:5, "Not by works of righteousness which we have done, but according to his mercy he saved us, by the washing of regeneration, and renewing of the Holy Ghost"; and 2 Thess. 2:13, "But we are bound to give thanks to God always for you, brethren beloved of the Lord, because God hath from the beginning chosen you to salvation through sanctification of the Spirit and belief of the truth."

Both justification and sanctification are purchased at the cost of Christ's shed blood on Calvary's cross: Rom. 5:9, "Much more then, being now justified by his blood, we shall be saved from wrath through him"; and Heb. 13:12, "Wherefore Jesus also, that he might sanctify the people with his own blood, suffered without the gate."

Both justification and sanctification are brought to the individual believer's heart in response to faith: Rom. 5:1, "Therefore being justified by faith, we have peace with God through our Lord Jesus Christ"; and Acts 26:18, "To open their eyes, and to turn them from darkness to light, and from the power of Satan unto God, that they may receive the forgiveness of sins, and inheritance among them that are sanctified by faith that is in me."

Now, virtually all Bible-believing Christians recognize that the new birth, justification, is not gradual, but instantaneous. It is an act of God that takes place at a given point in a believer's life. But if both justification and sanctification are products of the same divine love, the same will of God, the same Holy Word, the same blessed Spirit, the same redeeming Blood, and the same human condition—faith—is there any valid reason for supposing that one is instantaneous while the other is gradual? If justification is instantaneous, there is certainly no reason why sanctification, wrought by the same agency, should not be equally the act of a moment.

> EVERY ARGUMENT THAT PROVES THE INSTANTANEOUSNESS OF REGENERATION IS JUST AS FORCEFUL WHEN APPLIED TO SANCTIFICATION.

As a matter of fact, every argument that proves the instantaneousness of regeneration is just as forceful when applied to sanctification. If the evidence for the immediacy of sanctification be rejected, there is no logical ground on which to base proof for the immediacy of justification.

2. *The Testimony of the Terms.* We next look briefly at the terms used to describe this second work in the Christian heart. Without exception, the root action is such as to imply that which occurs at a particular point in time.

The verb "to sanctify" is defined in its twofold meaning as "to set apart" and "to make holy." There may, it is true, be a gradual setting apart, a gradual making holy. But the action described is much more naturally thought of as momentary and immediate. Since "to sanctify" in its strictly New Testament sense is always spoken of as a divine act, the burden of proof ought naturally to rest upon those who allege sanctification to be gradual.

Then, this experience is spoken of as a baptism: "John truly baptized with water, but ye shall be baptized with the Holy Ghost not many days hence" (Acts

1:5). Baptism is a term that always implies action at a given point—never that which is drawn out over a long period of time, and perhaps never completed until death. Gradual baptism is an absurdity—whether it be a baptism with water or the baptism with the Holy Spirit.

It is spoken of as a crucifixion or death. Rom. 6:6: "Knowing this, that our old man is crucified with him, that the body of sin might be destroyed, that henceforth we should not serve sin." Gal. 2:20: "I am crucified with Christ: nevertheless I live; yet not I, but Christ liveth in me: and the life which I now live in the flesh, I live by the faith of the Son of God, who loved me, and gave himself for me." Col. 3:5: "Mortify [treat as dead] therefore your members which are upon the earth."

It may be granted that one may be long a-dying, but death always occurs in a moment. Life may wane over a period of time, but it departs the body at a given instant. Gradual death is a figure of speech for a mortal illness. Death itself is always instantaneous.

Sanctification involves cleansing, purifying. The verses quoted in chapter 1 are replete with uses of the verbs "cleanse," "purify." Cleansing and purification may be continuous processes, but the natural meaning of these words indicates that there is always an initial moment when the cleansing and purification is first accomplished. To make it gradual is to read into it something that the words themselves certainly do not imply.

> **THE GRADUAL GIVING OF A GIFT IS A CONFUSION OF TERMS.**

This experience is described as a "gift" to be "received." "The gift of the Holy Ghost" is frequently mentioned throughout the New Testament, often as "the promise of the Father." Jesus, in Luke 11:13, said, "If ye, then, being evil, know how to give good gifts unto your children: how much more shall your heavenly Father give the Holy Spirit to them that ask him?" Gal. 3:14, "That we might receive the promise of the Spirit through faith." Is it not obvious that a gift is something that passes into the possession of its receiver at some given moment? The gradual giving of a gift is a confusion of terms.

We could go on at length. Sanctification is variously described as putting off the old man and putting on the new (Eph. 4:20-24); it is destroying the body of sin (Rom. 6:6); it is being filled with the Spirit (Eph. 5:18); it is to be sealed with that Holy Spirit of promise (Eph. 1:13).

To summarize: "to set apart," "to make holy," "to baptize," "to crucify," "to put to death," "to give," "to receive," "to put off," "to put on," "to destroy," "to be filled," "to be sealed"—these are all verbs describing actions that take place most naturally at a definite time and place, and which do not admit of degrees. They all testify to the fact that sanctification is a crisis experience, not a long-drawn-out and never-completed process of growth.

**3. *The Logic of Example.*** There is a final line of evidence for the instantaneousness of entire sanctification, based upon scriptural examples of this grace.

The experience of Isaiah recorded in Isa. 6 may be regarded as a type of the believer's experience of entire sanctification. Isaiah had been a prophet of God during part of the reign of King Uzziah, as he tells us in chapter 1. But it was in the year the king died that God's prophet experienced his remarkable cleansing.

In the Temple worshiping, Isaiah saw the Lord "high and lifted up" and heard the seraphs' song, "Holy, holy, holy, is the LORD of hosts." That praise of God's holiness found no echo in the prophet's heart, and he who had previously called woes on the people now cried out again for himself, "Woe is me! for I am undone; because I am a man of unclean lips, and I dwell in the midst of a people of unclean lips."

But the divine response was not long in coming. An angel flew with golden tongs and a live coal from the altar, touched his lips, and said, "Lo, this hath touched thy lips; and thine iniquity is taken away, and thy sin purged." This all took place in less time than it takes to describe. It was not by growth or spiritual development that Isaiah's iniquity was taken away and his sin purged. It was by a divine act at a given time.

In the New Testament, all examples of the baptism with the Spirit and entire sanctification are found in the Book of Acts. They are four in number.

The first involves the disciples of Jesus, whose names were written in heaven (Luke 10:20); who were not of the world (John 14:16-17; 17:14); who belonged to Christ (John 17:6, 11); not one of whom was lost (John 17:12); and who had kept God's words (John 17:6). While these clearly justified persons "were all of one accord in one place . . . suddenly there came a sound from heaven as of a rushing mighty wind . . . and they were all filled with the Holy Ghost" (Acts 2:1-4). There was no gradual growing into this. It came with the unexpected suddenness of lightning from the skies.

The second example found in the Book of Acts was recorded of the young church in Samaria. Philip had ventured into Samaria after the martyrdom of Stephen. His preaching met with a ready response. The people believed and were baptized in large numbers. Acts 8:8 records that "there was great joy in that city."

Hearing of this revival and the success of the ministry of the Word, the apostles at Jerusalem sent Peter and John to Samaria. When they came, they prayed for these young converts, "that they might receive the Holy Ghost: (for as yet he was fallen upon none of them: only they were baptized in the name of the Lord Jesus). Then laid they their hands on them, and they received the Holy Ghost" (Acts 8:15-17).

It is sometimes fashionable to reject the example of the disciples of Christ as not truly typical because they lived under two dispensations. Thus, it is claimed, Pentecost was in effect the completion of their regeneration, and every believer now receives the baptism with the Holy Spirit at the moment he first receives Christ as his Savior. This argument is refuted by the example of the Samaritan church. The Samaritans believed and were baptized in the new dispensation of the Spirit, and they were afterward filled with the Holy Ghost at a given instant of time.

The third example concerns the devout Roman centurion Cornelius, and members of his household. Cornelius is described in clear terms by God's inspired penman. He was a devout man (Acts 10:2). He feared God with all his house (Acts 10:2). He prayed constantly, and his prayers were accepted by God (Acts 10:2, 4). Peter, arriving at Cornelius' house, with quick spiritual insight said:

> Of a truth, I perceive that God is no respecter of persons: but in every nation he that feareth him, and worketh righteousness, is accepted with him. The word which God sent unto the children of Israel, preaching peace by Jesus Christ: (he is Lord of all:) that word, I say, ye know, which was published throughout all Judaea" (Acts 10:34-37).

As Peter continued to speak, suddenly the Holy Spirit fell on those who listened. This was not gradual, but instantaneous. That Peter himself regarded the events at Cornelius' home as parallel with and identical to the events at Pentecost is clearly seen in his report to the council at Jerusalem: God, knowing their hearts, bore witness and gave the Holy Spirit, even as He had at Pentecost, purifying their hearts by faith (Acts 15:8-9).[2]

The fourth instance given in the Book of Acts is described in 18:24—19:7. It concerns the disciples at Ephesus. Because there has been so much misunderstanding connected with this episode, it is necessary to go into the background a bit more extensively.

At the end of the apostle Paul's long ministry in Corinth, he, in company with Aquila and Priscilla, his co-laborers, crossed the Aegean Sea to the mainland of Asia and the city of Ephesus. Paul himself spent only a brief time preaching in the synagogue at Ephesus and, leaving Aquila and Priscilla there, he went on toward Antioch.

While Paul was gone, a man named Apollos came to Ephesus. Apollos is described as eloquent, mighty in the Scriptures, instructed in the way of the Lord, and speaking and teaching diligently the things of the Lord, although, as far as baptism was concerned, he knew only the baptism of John. Recognizing the potential greatness of Apollos' ministry, Aquila and Priscilla took him and taught him the way of God more perfectly (Acts 18:24-28).

Shortly after Apollos left his newfound friends to go to Corinth, Paul came back to Ephesus. Whatever their origin, whether as converts of Aquila and Priscilla, or of Apollos, Paul found in Ephesus a nucleus of 12 disciples. Examining them, he learned that they had not received the Holy Ghost, at least in the measure of Pentecost. But after Paul had baptized them in the name of Christ, he prayed, laid hands upon them, and they were filled with the Holy Spirit.

The misunderstanding that surrounds this incident has to do with the spiritual status of the Ephesian disciples. Because they disclaimed knowledge of the Holy Spirit, and because they had received only the baptism of John, some have contended that they were unregenerate persons. That these 12 people were genuine children of God and that this was for them a second instantaneous experience, we firmly believe to be the teaching of this passage. Let us examine the important considerations here.

First, the men are described as disciples (Acts 19:1) and "the disciples were first called Christians at Antioch" (Acts 11:26). The designations "Christian" and "disciple" were used interchangeably in the Book of Acts. There is no other instance of the use of the term "disciple" in the Acts for any other than true believers in Christ.

Second, Paul did not challenge the fact of their faith. "Have ye received the Holy Ghost since ye believed?" he asked them (Acts 19:2). Whether the original be translated as it is thus in the Authorized Version, or translated as it is in the American and Revised Standard Versions, "Did you receive the Holy Spirit when you believed?" makes not the slightest bit of difference so far as this point is concerned. In either case, it is admitted that they had believed, and it is evident that they had not received the Holy Ghost in the sense in which Paul speaks.

Third, that they were ignorant of the receiving of the Holy Spirit does not mean that they had not been converted. Dwight L. Moody asserted that for many years after his conversion he did not know that the Holy Spirit was a Person, and that many believers today are as ignorant of the person and ministry of the Holy Spirit as were these Ephesian believers.[3]

Fourth, that these men had only the baptism of John does not prove that they were unconverted in the full Christian sense of the word. In fact, the baptism of John is spoken of as a "baptism of repentance for the remission of sins" (Mark 1:4). Apollos, instructed in the way of the Lord, fervent in the Spirit, speaking and teaching diligently the things of the Lord, knew only the baptism of John.

Fifth, that Paul was satisfied with the faith of these disciples is seen in the fact that he rebaptized them in the name of the Lord Jesus Christ before they were filled with the Holy Spirit. If they were only at that time being regenerated in the Christian sense, then Paul was guilty of baptizing a group of unconverted men. That such has often been done since, we will not debate; but that Paul began the practice in Ephesus, we cannot admit.

Finally, that "receiving" the Holy Spirit refers to something more than being born again by the Spirit and led by the Spirit is testified to by no less authority than the Lord Jesus himself. In John 14:15-17, we read:

> If ye love me, keep my commandments. And I will pray the Father and he shall give you another Comforter, that he may abide with you for ever;

even the Spirit of truth; whom the world cannot receive, because it seeth him not, neither knoweth him: but ye know him; for he dwelleth with you, and shall be in you.

Here Jesus indicates clearly that the world, and those who are of the world, cannot receive the Holy Spirit. One must *know* Him before *receiving* Him. One must have the Spirit *with* him before he can have the Spirit *in* him. While the phrase "receive the Holy Spirit" is used only four times in the New Testament (John 14:17; Acts 8:15-17; Acts 19:2; and Gal. 3:14), in each case it is made clear that it is the believer alone who is in a position to *receive* the Holy Spirit. We should not put too much weight on the argument from analogy, but it is surely no accident that the inspired writers of the New Testament chose the figures *birth of the Spirit* to represent regeneration and *baptism with the Spirit* to describe the "second blessing." Obviously, in the order of nature, birth *must* precede baptism—a child has to be born before he can be baptized.

> **EACH INSTANCE WAS CHARACTERIZED BY IMMEDIACY.**

Here then is the logic of example. Each instance was characterized by immediacy. Each took place at a given point in the experience of the persons involved. Nowhere is there a trace of sanctification by growth, a long process of self-discipline, never completed until the rapture. If it is of faith, then it is "not of works, lest any man should boast" (Rom. 11:6; Eph. 2:9).

## THE TESTIMONY OF THE TENSES

There is another impressive line of evidence leading to acceptance of the instantaneousness of sanctification that is of particular interest to the one who has some acquaintance with Greek grammar. A most persuasive summary of this argument is to be found in the article by Dr. Daniel Steele, included in his *Milestone Papers,* titled "The Tense Readings of the Greek New Testament."[4]

The main point in this argument lies in the fact that the tenses of the Greek verb have a somewhat different significance from those of the English. Our verb tenses have to do mainly with the *time* of action—past, present, or future. Greek tenses do denote time, but more particularly the *kind* of action. This is, the action may be viewed as a continuing process, known as *linear* action; or it may be viewed as a whole in what is known as momentary or *punctiliar* action. Thus, continued action or a state of incompleteness is denoted by the present and imperfect tenses in the Greek. On the other hand, point-action, which is momentary or punctiliar, is expressed by the consistent use of the aorist tense. William Hersey Davis says, *"The aorist tense itself always means point-action."*[5]

The aorist refers to actions "thought of merely as events or single facts without reference to the time they occupied."[6] With the exception of the indicative aorist, which denotes past action, aorist forms are undefined as to time.

They all represent punctiliar as opposed to linear action. They describe completed, epochal events, treated as a totality. The aorist, says Afford, implies a definite act.[7]

The relevance of all this to our present subject is seen in the following quotation from Dr. Steele in the paper referred to earlier. Speaking of the findings of his study of the use of verb tenses in key New Testament passages, he says:

1. All exhortations to prayer and to spiritual endeavor in resistance of temptation are usually expressed in the present tense, which strongly indicates persistence. . . .

2. The next fact which impresses us in our investigation is *the absence of the aorist and the presence of the present tense whenever the conditions of final salvation are stated.* Our inference is that the conditions of ultimate salvation are continuous, extending through probation, and not completed in any one act. The great requirement is faith in Jesus Christ. A careful study of the Greek will convince the student that it is a great mistake to teach that a single act of faith furnishes a person with a paid-up, nonforfeitable policy assuring the holder that he will inherit eternal life, or that a single energy of faith secures a through ticket for heaven, as is taught by the Plymouth Brethren and by some popular lay evangelists. The Greek tenses show that faith is a state, a habit of mind, into which the believer enters at justification. . . .

3. But when we come to consider the *work of purification* in the believer's soul, by the power of the Holy Spirit, both in the new birth and in entire sanctification, we find that *the aorist is almost uniformly used.* This tense, according to the best New Testament grammarians, never indicates a continuous, habitual, or repeated act, but one which is momentary and done once for all.[8]

We have looked in vain to find one of these verbs (denoting sanctification and perfection) in the imperfect tense when individuals are spoken of. The verb *hagiazo*, to sanctify, is always aorist or perfect. . . . The same may be said of the verbs *katharizo* and *hagnizo*, to purify. Our inference is that the energy of the Holy Spirit in the work of entire sanctification, however long the preparation, is put forth at a stroke by a momentary act. This is corroborated by the universal testimony of those who have experienced this grace.[9]

It was Dr. E. F. Walker who pointed out years ago that, in the final analysis, all theories of sanctification must recognize its instantaneousness. If sanctification is at physical death, or at the resurrection, it must occur in an instant. Even if it be by growth, there must be a moment when full growth is attained. The debate centers about the issue as to when that completing instant occurs.

Here, we affirm, the testimony of God's Word is final. The hour of full salvation is not some remote future hour. The day of deliverance from all vestige of carnal sin is not some far-off day. Every divine imperative, every command of God is for the present moment, never for the future. "Behold, now is the accepted time; behold, now is the day of salvation" (2 Cor. 6:2).

1. Lewis Sperry Chafer, *Systematic Theology* (Dallas: Dallas Seminary Press, 1947), VI, 284-85.

2. The climaxing fullness of the Spirit was accepted by the Jerusalem church as convincing evidence that Gentiles were also "granted repentance unto life" (Acts 11:18). "Saved" as in Acts 11:14 is not a synonym of "converted," but includes God's total redemptive work in the heart.

3. Dwight L. Moody, *Secret Power* (Chicago: Bible Institute Colportage Association, 1908), 16, 50.

4. Daniel Steele, "The Tense Readings of the Greek New Testament," *Milestone Papers* (New York: Easton and Mains, 1878), 53-90. This has recently been reprinted in an appendix to Charles Ewing Brown, *The Meaning of Sanctification.* A more complete summation has been made by Drs. Olive M. Winchester and Ross E. Price in their book, *Crisis Experiences in the Greek New Testament* (Kansas City: Beacon Hill Press, 1953).

5. William Hersey Davis, *Beginner's Grammar of the Greek New Testament* (New York: George Doran Co., 1923), 123 (italics in original).

6. Hadley, *Greek Grammar for Schools and Colleges,* quoted by Winchester and Price, *Crisis Experiences.*

7. Quoted by Winchester and Price, *Crisis Experiences.*

8. Steele, *Milestone Papers,* 57, 59, 65-66.

9. Ibid., 90.

Originally published as chapter 2 of *Conflicting Concepts of Holiness,* rev. ed. (Kansas City: Nazarene Publishing House, 1972), 22-36.

Sanctification is God at work

in our lives:

shaping our characters,

tutoring our minds,

strengthening our wills,

and enabling us to satisfy

His demands

and fulfill our potential

as His children.

—James Earl Massey

From "What Sanctification Means" in *Great Holiness Classics, Vol. 5: Holiness Preachers and Preaching,* W. E. McCumber, ed. (Kansas City: Beacon Hill Press of Kansas City, 1989), 168.

# 7

# CONSECRATION: HOLY AND HIS
## —A Total Sellout to Self—

## Frank M. Moore

## Biblical Foundation

"May God himself, the God of peace, sanctify you through and through. May your whole spirit, soul and body be kept blameless at the coming of our Lord Jesus Christ. The one who calls you is faithful and he will do it" (1 Thess. 5:23-24, NIV).

"I urge you, brothers, in view of God's mercy, to offer your bodies as living sacrifices, holy and pleasing to God—this is your spiritual act of worship. Do not conform any longer to the pattern of this world, but be transformed by the renewing of your mind. Then you will be able to test and approve what God's will is—his good, pleasing and perfect will" (Rom. 12:1-2, NIV).

Jesus spoke often about being totally sold out to God. He said becoming a Christian is like selling all you have and taking the money to buy a valuable pearl. Or it's like taking all your money to buy a piece of property that has buried treasure on it. Jesus told the rich young ruler that he needed to sell his possessions and follow Him. Jesus did not oppose owning possessions, but He was opposed to them becoming our gods. Being the person God wants us to be requires a total sell-out.

## The Truth Explained in Everyday Language

The Christian journey begins the moment we ask Christ into our lives. It continues until we go to be with the Lord forever. As we grow and develop in our faith, God opens new doors of commitment through which we walk. Entire sanctification is one of those new doors.

The Bible often speaks of sanctification, which basically means the total, lifelong process of becoming holy. Because the process begins with the new birth, we call the spiritual growth immediately following regeneration "initial sanctification." That is, we begin walking God's way. The fruit of the Spirit in our lives becomes evidence that a change has taken place.

This process of spiritual growth may continue for months or even years before we sense a need for something more in our Christian journey. The common experience of saints down through the ages has been an awareness of a remaining hindrance to further spiritual progress. No outward sin—just an uncertain gnawing for something more. This awareness usually takes the form of an internal battle with the self, such as Paul described in Gal. 5:16-26. In summary he said, "The sinful nature desires what is contrary to the Spirit, and the Spirit what is contrary to the sinful nature. They are in conflict with each other, so that you do not do what you want" (v. 17, NIV).

> **THE BATTLE MAY BE SELF-CENTEREDNESS IN THE FORM OF SELF-SEEKING, SELF-ASSERTION, SELF-INDULGENCE, SELF-SUFFICIENCY, OR SELF-WILL.**

The battle may be self-centeredness in the form of self-seeking, self-assertion, self-indulgence, self-sufficiency, or self-will—all as a preference over God or others. It's not that we don't wish to please God—we do. Our problem involves wanting the best of both worlds, having what God wants *and* what we want at the same time. We realize we cannot have it both ways. We have been plagued with this problem since the Fall in the Garden of Eden.

Once we pinpoint the self-centeredness, we realize it must be replaced with Christ-centeredness. We confess our need to God and surrender ourselves completely to His will. The old-timers called it "dying out to self." They did not mean self-extinction or psychological suicide; rather, they meant self-preference replaced with God-preference. After full surrender comes faith in God to change us. We trust God to accept our consecration and fill us completely with His Holy Spirit. The Spirit entered our life when we accepted Christ; now we are inviting Him to take charge of our control center.

Entire sanctification is God's gift. We do not earn or deserve it any more than we earned or deserved regeneration. We consecrate; God sanctifies. So the two experiences of grace are similar in that we ask in faith and God grants us His gift. The two differ in a number of important ways, however. In regeneration we come to God as a rebel; in entire sanctification we come as a child of God seeking a deeper commitment. In regeneration we repent of wrongdoing; in entire sanctification we consecrate our wills and lives for all God wants to do with us. In regeneration we come with the guilt of a sinful lifestyle; in entire sanctification we come with the frustration and hindrance of a sin principle that causes us to prefer self.

Biblical terminology indicates that entire sanctification happens in a moment of time. Symbols include a baptism (Acts 1:5), a sealing (2 Cor. 1:22), a crucifixion (Rom. 6:6), and a circumcision (Col. 2:11). None of these symbols suggest a long process. Verb usage in the original language also indicates an immediate experience. For example, the Greek aorist tense suggests an event occurring at a moment in time. Nevertheless, the immediate experience must give way to a lifetime of growth in grace. The difference between our spiritual progress before and after entire sanctification centers on the removal of the hindrance of self-sovereignty. We now have a new openness to God's direction in our lives.

Just prior to Jesus' ascension back to heaven from the Mount of Olives, He told His disciples, "You will receive power when the Holy Spirit comes on you; and you will be my witnesses in Jerusalem, and in all Judea and Samaria, and to the ends of the earth" (Acts 1:8, NIV). The apostle Peter summarized the lasting results of entire sanctification when he spoke to the Jerusalem Council, comparing the events at Cornelius' house with Pentecost. He said, "God, who

**THE LASTING RESULTS OF ENTIRE SANCTIFICATION ARE POWER AND PURITY.**

knows the heart, showed that he accepted them by giving the Holy Spirit to them, just as he did to us. He made no distinction between us and them, for he purified their hearts by faith" (15:8-9, NIV). Together these two passages remind us that the lasting results of entire sanctification are power and purity.

Some refer to entire sanctification as "Christian perfection." Many people don't like that term because they misunderstand it to mean the entirely sanctified believe they are perfect. John Wesley also did not like the term for that reason. He continued to use it, however, because it's biblical. Jesus said. "Be perfect, therefore, as your heavenly Father is perfect" (Matt. 5:48, NIV). Since we are still human and continue to make mistakes and fall short of a perfect standard of conduct, what kind of "perfect" are we talking about? We mean perfect in motive and desire to please God. Our actions are not flawless but our intentions are pure. We want to please God more than anything else in the world. Thus, as Mother Teresa saw it, it is "doing the will of God with a smile." Years of maturity and growth will bring our performance more into line with the desires of our heart. God's Spirit continues to work with us to complete that process.

## Using the Truth to Enrich Your Life

Recently Sue and I visited our friends Chip and Dana in southern California. Dana showed us to the guest bedroom and said, "Make yourselves at home." Now, she didn't really mean it. She meant we had their permission to hang our clothes in the closet and spread our personal items around the bedroom. She also meant we could use the iron or eat food from the kitchen. But that's about it. When I'm at our home, I can move the furniture, hang up new pictures, and even knock out a wall if I want to enlarge a room. I doubt if our friends would have appreciated our rearranging their living room furniture or conducting a garage sale of their possessions.

Something like our California visit exists in our relationship with God. We invite Him into our lives when we become a Christian. He is a guest in our hearts. He has control of us—within the limits we set. Our lives reflect His presence in ways people can see. In time, however, we begin to sense some resistance on our part to His additional resources for more control. We liked it just fine when His presence brought us peace and joy. Now He seems to be going a little too far by asking more than we care to give, like an Internal Revenue Service agent going through our financial records and wanting more tax money.

> GOD'S FULL CONTROL IS THE MOST LIBERATING WAY TO LIVE.

God wants full control of our entire being. It comes down to a question of who is going to call the shots in life—us or God. If we retain control, we hinder further spiritual growth; the relationship suffers. If we give Him control, we fear He might ask us to do something we don't want to do, like becoming a missionary to Bugville or shaving our head. Then we wouldn't be happy. Nonsense. That is Satan's lie. God's full control is the most liberating way to live. It is a blessed abandonment of self-interest. God always has our best interest in mind, and He seeks to do more in us than we ever dreamed possible. That's what makes entire sanctification the greatest adventure in our spiritual journey. Giving God everything pays dividends for all of eternity.

Originally published as "Holy and His," chapter 13 of *More Coffee Shop Theology* (Kansas City: Beacon Hill Press of Kansas City, 1991), 67-71.

We are persuaded

that there is no end to the

possibilities of a soul in grace.

The love of God

is measureless,

and we may even know

more and more of His

boundless grace. . . . But

entire sanctification

is not obtained by growth.

—Phineas F. Bresee

From *The Quotable Bresee,* Harold Ivan Smith, comp. (Kansas City: Beacon Hill Press of Kansas City, 1983), 35.

# 8

# SANCTIFICATION: ENJOYING THE DOCTRINE IN EXPERIENCE

## —How the Holiness Doctrine Operates in Human Life—

## H. Ray Dunning

IT IS ONE THING to read and study a doctrine. It is something much richer and much more satisfying to enjoy that doctrine in experience. Thus it is important to attempt to understand how the biblical teaching about sanctification applies to daily life.

Perhaps the first step is to explore what the Bible says about experience. But before we can do that, we must try to define what the term *experience* means.

For our purposes in this chapter, we will use *experience* to refer to the manner in which sanctifying grace operates in human life, how it is actualized in our daily, down-to-earth existence. The first question then is, Is there a revealed pattern of this divine action?

It is important to recognize that the Bible does not lay down a stereotyped answer to this question. We may find hints concerning our role in the process, but none of these suggests a formula that can become a ritual. One reason for this is that sanctification is the work of God, and He cannot be forced into a box. Another is the irreducible variety of religious experiences. It is true that some spiritual leaders have laid down "steps to sanctification" and attempted to describe the manner in which God works, but this raises a real danger of creating clones of their personal experience and fails to recognize the sovereignty of God as well as the influence of many forces on the shape of experience. In addition, the Bible does not prescribe a pattern of how God invariably works in human life. It basically describes the state of humanity in sin and sets forth the goal of God's redemptive process but does not specify the specific route by which one would arrive there.

John Wesley is at his best when he discusses this aspect of sanctification.

He recognized the truth that the Bible is silent on the manner, and he attempted to examine the experiences of as many people as he could who claimed to have experienced the grace of entire sanctification. By this method he came to conclusions about how God *normally* worked but not how He *must* work. What did he discover by this inductive method?

## INSTANTANEOUS AND LIFELONG PROCESS

**THE DISTINCTIVE THAT WESLEY DISCOVERED IN THE EXPERIENCE OF MANY WAS THAT THERE WAS THE POSSIBILITY OF DELIVERANCE FROM ALL SIN *IN THIS LIFE* AND THAT THIS STAGE OF GRACE OCCURS IN A MOMENT OF TIME.**

He learned that sanctification is a lifelong process that includes an instantaneous moment at which one is perfected in love. To this moment he gave the term *entire sanctification* or *Christian perfection*, or *full salvation*. This moment occurs when God delivers the believer from all sin.

Wesley also discovered from experience what was quite explicit in the structure of the New Testament: No one had experienced full deliverance from inward sin at the moment of initial salvation. While it may not have been apparent at first due to the joy and victory of conversion, eventually all became aware of remaining sin (self-centeredness).

Scriptural support for the lifelong process is not difficult to establish since the New Testament references to the Christian life are dominantly in the present progressive tense in the original Greek. This Mr. Wesley understood as that gradual renewal in the image of God that begins in the new birth and continues until death—and beyond.

Because of this *obvious* teaching of Scripture, the whole-life developmental aspect of sanctification has been recognized by almost all Christian teachers. But the distinctive that Wesley discovered in the experience of many was that there was the possibility of deliverance from all sin *in this life* and that this stage of grace occurs in a moment of time.

## WESLEY'S REASONS FOR BELIEVING IN THE CRISIS

He based his belief in the instantaneous character of entire sanctification on at least four grounds:

*1. It is done in response to faith.* Early in his experience, Wesley believed that this stage of grace occurred only late in life after a lengthy process of maturation. However, he came to see that since it is by faith, there is no reason why one should not claim this "blessing" early on in one's spiritual pilgrimage. Of course, he always deferred to the sovereignty of God and did not believe one should feel any sense of guilt if God had not chosen to effect the great inward transformation.

**2. Experience.** After carefully examining the testimonies of numerous persons, Wesley reached the conclusion that all had experienced the great transformation in an instant. True, this moment was both preceded and followed by gradual sanctification or growth in grace, but the actual deliverance from inward sin was instantaneous.

**3. Logic.** By drawing an analogy with the gradual approach of death, he demonstrated how there is a logical moment at which entire sanctification occurs. His own description of this reasoning is quite clear:

> A man may be dying for some time; yet he does not properly speaking, die, till the soul is separated from the body; and in that instant, he lives the life of eternity. In like manner, he may be dying to sin for some time; yet he is not dead to sin, till sin is separated from his soul; and in that instant, he lives the full life of love. And as the change undergone, when the body dies, is of a different kind, and infinitely greater than any we had known before, yea, such as till then, it is impossible to conceive; so the change wrought, when the soul dies to sin, is of a different kind, and infinitely greater than any before, and that any can conceive, till he experiences it. Yet he still grows in grace, in the knowledge of Christ, in the love and image of God; and will do so, not only till death, but through all eternity.[1]

> WESLEY EMPHASIZES THE CORRELATION OF MOMENT AND PROCESS, ALLOWING NEITHER TO DISAPPEAR FROM THE EXPERIENCE OF THE BELIEVER.

Here again we see how Wesley emphasizes the correlation of moment and process, allowing neither to disappear from the experience of the believer. The instant of entire sanctification is a point in a lifelong process.

**4. The nature of sin.** As we have seen, Wesley understood the nature of sin to be self-will. This, he argued, is the root of all sin. All acts that are sinful are expressions of this "seed." One must be careful not to be confused by the metaphors, "root" and "seed," and think of them as referring to some "thing" within the person. It is the universal bent of fallen humanity toward self-sovereignty that remains, though it does not reign, in believers.

It is in the light of this understanding of sin that Wesley's words have meaning. Since they are so precise and clear, we simply quote them:

> Although we may *weaken* our enemies day by day; yet we cannot *drive them out.* By all the grace which is given at justification we cannot extirpate them. Though we watch and pray ever so much, we cannot wholly cleanse either our hearts or hands. Most sure we cannot, till it shall please our Lord to speak to our hearts again, to speak the second time, "Be clean"; and then only, the leprosy is cleansed. Then only, the evil root, the carnal mind, is destroyed; and inbred sin subsists no more.[2]

Wesley was able to maintain a proper balance between the process and the moment, something many of his spiritual children have been unable to do. But if we are going to have a doctrine that is livable, both must be kept in view. I participated in a conference on church renewal in the Wesleyan holiness tradition. One of the papers was presented by General Superintendent Lee M. Haines of The Wesleyan Church, in which he said:

> We must renew our vision of sanctification as both a pilgrimage and an event, as a process and a relationship with a history, a healing and a healthy growth, a quest and a gift. We must not reduce sanctification to a single moment in time. Neither must we forget the importance of such a moment of commitment on our part and the bringing of wholeness on God's part, allowing all of that to be eroded away in the partial truth of gradual development. It has been extremely difficult for the followers of Wesley to maintain his synthesis of the event and the process. The pendulum has swung widely from one extreme to another, and is still swinging at the present time. But if the renewal movement is to be renewed, we must honestly face the paradox of a moment and a lifetime, both of which are necessary if we are to be holy as he is holy.

If we diagram the Christian life, we run the risk of creating a stereotype such as we have spoken against. Yet, with its limitations, such a picture can give us some insight into a normal development of grace in human life. The late Bishop Leslie R. Marston of the Free Methodist Church spoke in a Wesleyan Theology Conference about the preaching he had heard while growing up in the church and referred to it as the "plateau concept." As I recall my early experience of holiness preaching, it generally reflected the same pattern. Bishop Marston diagramed it like this:

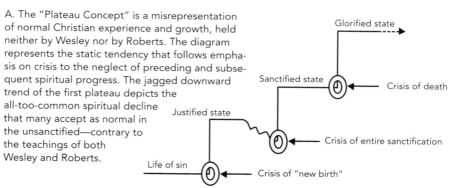

A. The "Plateau Concept" is a misrepresentation of normal Christian experience and growth, held neither by Wesley nor by Roberts. The diagram represents the static tendency that follows emphasis on crisis to the neglect of preceding and subsequent spiritual progress. The jagged downward trend of the first plateau depicts the all-too-common spiritual decline that many accept as normal in the unsanctified—contrary to the teachings of both Wesley and Roberts.

Glorified state

Sanctified state — Crisis of death

Justified state

Crisis of entire sanctification

Life of sin — Crisis of "new birth"

He then talked about the view of the Christian life that he had found presented in the writings of Benjamin T. Roberts (founder of the Free Methodist Church). When I heard his presentation at the conference, I was very excited, because it was almost precisely the understanding I had derived from an intensive study of John Wesley's teaching, and I had used substantially the same diagram in my own teaching. Bishop Marston's representation looked like this:

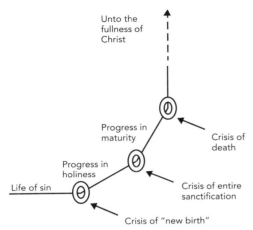

B. The "Dynamic Concept" of Christian experience and growth prevails in the teachings of both Wesley and Roberts, emphasizing progress between crises. Roberts, however, conceived of Christian perfection as the normal progress of every fully obedient and believing Christian, whereas Wesley identified Christian perfection with entire sanctification.

NOTE: In both diagrams the coiled-spring symbol at points of crisis is intended to indicate that the direction of growth changes in consequence of an inner work of divine grace.

These charts accompany and are a part of "The Crisis-Process Issue in Wesleyan Thought," a paper presented before the Wesleyan Theological Society at Olivet Nazarene College, November 2, 1968, by Leslie N. Marston.

This approach to the Christian life is far more exciting and truer to a biblical picture than the first. The beauty of it is that it integrates progressive and instantaneous sanctification in a fashion that is consistent with the way life is lived out.

The shape of the moment of experience we call entire sanctification is influenced by a number of factors: personality, environment, culture, socioeconomic status, and no doubt many others. For some persons, that moment is marked by a traumatic struggle with surrender to the will of God as they understand it. In their case it becomes a real crisis. For others, it is a gentle transition perhaps hardly noticeable at its passing because they are simply walking on in the sincere quest for the fullness of God. The difference in the character of the experience does not in any case invalidate its reality.

Dr. Daniel Steele, early scholar in the holiness movement and professor at Boston University, recognized this truth and gave wise counsel to the young minister who was leaving the classroom for the parish.

We learn from books and from the lectures of some theological professors that both regeneration and entire sanctification are states of grace sharply defined, entered upon instantaneously after certain definite steps, and followed by certain very marked results. But the young preacher soon learns that there are eminently spiritual members of his church whose experiences have not been in accordance with this regulation manner. They have passed through no marked and memorable crises. Hence they have no spiritual anniversaries. The young pastor is puzzled by these anomalies. At last, if he is wise he will conclude that the books describe normal experiences to which the Holy Spirit does not limit itself, and that an abnormal method of gaining a spiritual change or elevation is by no means to be discounted.[3]

> GOD RESPECTS OUR INDIVIDUALITY AND DOES NOT SQUEEZE US INTO A FORM OF RELIGIOUS EXPRESSION THAT VIOLATES AND THUS IN A SENSE DESTROYS OUR UNIQUENESS.

The American holiness movement emerged in the midst of a cultural situation that accentuated highly emotional religious experiences. Evangelism in this setting as it was practiced in the frontier camp meeting and the protracted meeting resulted in varied and unusual demonstrations, and vocal praise to God. When holiness evangelists took over the methods of the revivalists, the same responses were generated as persons came to the "mourner's bench" to seek entire sanctification. These were all valid expressions of genuine religious experience. Many persons today still find fulfillment and meaning in this form of religious expression. But other personality types, and socio-cultural-economic development have led equally devout and religious people to experience sanctifying grace in less dramatic ways, though just as real and transforming. It seems important to recognize for oneself as well as others that God respects our individuality and does not squeeze us into a form of religious expression that violates and thus in a sense destroys our uniqueness.

Many sincere persons have left the holiness movement simply because strong personalities have attempted to foist their own type of experience upon others. When they could not conform to these types of experience, they sought an environment less oppressive. We should be mature enough to recognize that God allows each one of us to be ourselves within the context of the sanctifying work of the Holy Spirit.

## PREPARING FOR THE HOLY SPIRIT'S SANCTIFYING WORK

How do we prepare to receive God's sanctifying grace? As we have said before, there are no magic formulas that lead automatically into the relation called entire sanctification. But there are some clues from Scripture and experience as to the kinds of things we must do.

In the Old Testament we noted how the ceremonial practices set persons or things apart for God's ownership or service. In fact, most emphasis is laid upon the human part, our sanctification of ourselves in this sense. No doubt this influences Paul's exhortation to those who have been justified, appealing to them to yield or present themselves to God. In Rom. 6:13 he says, "Offer yourselves to God, as those who have been brought from death to life; and offer the parts of your body to him as instruments of righteousness!" This is reiterated in verse 19 when he exhorts, "Now offer [the parts of your body] in slavery to righteousness leading to holiness!" (NIV).

The apostle Paul's point is that this is the logical thing to do. Now that one has been transported from being "in Adam" to being "in Christ" and become alive unto God, one should carry through the logical implications of that work of grace by this act of complete consecration. We may thus suggest that a full and complete consecration is one important element in appropriating the grace of entire sanctification.

## REPENTANCE, MORTIFICATION, AND GLORIFICATION

John Wesley generally speaks about three aspects of one's purposeful pursuit of full salvation. The first of these is *repentance.* This is different from the first repentance that precedes and prepares for saving faith. It basically involves two matters: self-knowledge and awareness of one's inability to cleanse oneself from remaining sin.

This suggests that a sense of need is fundamental to receiving God's sanctifying grace. When one becomes conscious of this inward disposition to self-sovereignty that is referred to in the New Testament as carnal mindedness or "the flesh," the way is prepared to cry out to God for deliverance. Alongside of this consciousness is the equally important sense that our own strength is incapable of overcoming it or putting it to death.

Then comes *mortification,* meaning the putting away of the marks of the old life and by means of spiritual exercises and discipline seeking to bring our lives into conformity to God's will. This seems to imply a gradual elimination of manifestations of self-centered behavior. The final step is *faith,* which is the appropriation of the promises of God. Faith answers to the second aspect of repentance and recognizes our complete dependence upon the work of the Spirit to cleanse away the remnants of sin (self-will) that are present in the born-again believer.

Alongside these special considerations, Wesley emphasized the practice of those regular Christian disciplines: prayer, Bible reading, worship, partaking of the sacraments and other means of grace. All these further the work of sanctification in human life, not only leading to the stage of perfect love but also enhancing the Christian life to its climax in glorification.

## HOMESICK FOR HOLINESS

The clearest statement of a doctrine of Christian experience is worthless unless accompanied by a hunger for the reality. The tragedy of history is that most religious movements that began with an all-consuming passion for "the simplicity and spiritual power of the primitive New Testament church" eventually became organizations preoccupied with their own existence. The initial impulse faded, and the ideals of the fathers became crystallized into dogma without life.

It is my earnest desire that you will find a new depth of understanding of the doctrine of sanctification. But I have a more burning desire that the reader will know the "hungering and thirsting after righteousness" that will pursue the ideal, will experience that "homesickness for holiness" that has marked sincere souls throughout Christian history.

If one analyzes the Wesley hymns, he will sense the desire for fullness that no doubt was the life breath of that movement in its prime. The aspiration for holiness comes to poetic expression in many ways. Let's close with a few verses from one of these hymns of aspiration, accompanied by a heart-felt prayer that they may become our prayer.

> *Love divine, all loves excelling,*
> *Joy of heav'n, to earth come down!*
> *Fix in us Thy humble dwelling;*
> *All Thy faithful mercies crown.*
>
> *Jesus, Thou art all compassion;*
> *Pure, unbounded love Thou art.*
> *Visit us with Thy salvation;*
> *Enter ev'ry trembling heart.*
>
> *Finish then Thy new creation;*
> *Pure and spotless let us be.*
> *Let us see Thy great salvation,*
> *Perfectly restored in Thee.*
>
> *Changed from glory into glory,*
> *Till in heav'n we take our place,*
> *Till we cast our crowns before Thee,*
> *Lost in wonder, love, and praise.*
> —Charles Wesley

---

1. John Wesley, *A Plain Account of Christian Perfection* (Kansas City: Beacon Hill Press of Kansas City, 1968), 62.

2. John Wesley, *The Standard Sermons of John Wesley*, 2 vols., ed. E. H. Sugden (London: Epworth Press, 1961), 2:390-91.

3. Daniel Steele, *Steele's Answers* (Chicago: Christian Witness Co., 1912), 128.

Originally published as chapter 8 and epilogue of *A Layman's Guide to Sanctification* (Kansas City: Beacon Hill Press of Kansas City, 1991), 71-81, 89-90.

Always remember

the essence of

Christian holiness

is simplicity and purity:

one design, one desire:

entire devotion

to God.

—John Wesley

From *Through the Year with Wesley,* Frederick Hill, ed. (Nashville: The Upper Room, 1983), 14.

# 9

# THE MIND OF CHRIST VS. THE CARNAL MIND

## —LIFE IN THE SPIRIT OR LIFE IN THE FLESH—

## Dennis F. Kinlaw

DO YOU FEEL there is a tug-of-war going on within you? Do you find yourself hesitating to do what God is calling you to do, because you feel there might be a more pleasant or more socially acceptable alternative? Do you feel guilty because you hold back from giving yourself fully to the Lord?

The divided heart is an agonizing state to live in. It's impossible for a person to stay there long; you will choose either God's way or the world's way. I've observed that the divided heart is a common experience among Christians. However, it is not the way that the New Testament calls us to live.

Romans 8 says,

> There is therefore now no condemnation for those who are in Christ Jesus. For the law of the Spirit of life in Christ Jesus has set you free from the law of sin and of death. For God has done what the law, weakened by the flesh, could not do: by sending his own Son in the likeness of sinful flesh, and to deal with sin, he condemned sin in the flesh, so that the just requirement of the law might be fulfilled in us, who walk not according to the flesh but according to the Spirit (vv. 1-4).[1]

Paul says the requirements of God's law can be fulfilled in the likes of you and me. He says the power of God can bring us to the point that we can please God himself.

Paul acknowledges that there are two ways people can attempt to please God. One way is to work out of our own resources. The other is to let God put his Spirit in us and fill us, so that we can live out of the resources of the Spirit. If we attempt to live out of our own resources, Paul says, we're living "according to the flesh." But if we live out of the resources of God, we live "according to the Spirit." Paul sees no third alternative. Ultimately you and I must live one way or the other. We must live "in the flesh" without God or we must live in the Spirit and be totally God's.

I am intrigued by the sharp contrast that Paul draws between the "flesh" and the Spirit. He makes very clear the disastrous consequences of "living in the flesh" and the glorious privileges of living in the Spirit. Notice what he says about living in "the flesh."

**THE FLESH SEES GOD AS THE ENEMY.**

First, he says that if you live "in the flesh," you will die. Verse 6 bluntly declares that "to set the mind (Greek, *phroneō*) on the flesh is death." Verse 13 reiterates, "If you live according to the flesh, you will die." Why? Because life is in God; it is not in us. So if we attempt to live on our own power and wisdom, we will perish.

Second, he says that if you try to live without God, you will be hostile to God. No one can remain neutral with regard to God's will. Notice verse 7: "For this reason the mind that is set on the flesh is hostile to God; it does not submit to God's law—indeed it cannot." Apart from the Holy Spirit's working in a person's life, that person will be hostile to God. The flesh sees God as the enemy. The perfect picture of demonstration of that fact is the Cross, where the likes of you and me murdered God when he came to live among us. Paul is setting up the sharply etched reality that there can be no middle ground between life "in the flesh" and life in the Spirit.

Third, he says that if you "live in the flesh," you cannot please God. Notice verse 8: "Those who are in the flesh cannot please God." So if human desire dominates my life, I will find a hostility rising in me against God. I will not please him. I will be separated from him. I have no option but death.

The fourth thing Paul says is that "living in the flesh" is to live in bondage. Look at verse 15: "For you did not receive a spirit of slavery to fall back into fear, but you have received a spirit of adoption." He's contrasting the Spirit of God and the spirit of human flesh, saying that the flesh is bondage. The natural man knows what it means to live in bondage. It may be a habit; it may be lust; it may be any manifestation of sin. Whatever form the bondage may take, a human being living in the flesh is powerless to rid himself/herself of sin. That bondage brings an ominous sense of fear. We know intuitively that we are not right, so we have a fear of God.

## LIFE IN THE SPIRIT

Now Paul shows us the opposite. "For the law of the Spirit of life in Christ Jesus has set you free from the law of sin and of death" (v. 2). Sin does not have to dominate us. Death does not have to determine our destiny. In fact, if you look at verse 4, you will even find that it is possible for a person like you and me to please God. The end result in verse 6 is that we have life and peace. We have the privilege of being led by the Holy Spirit. We can walk in the Spirit. We don't have to fear God because he puts a witness in our heart that we are his children and we belong to him. What an incredible experience it is when God tells you that you belong to him.

Then, as we walk with him, the Holy Spirit intercedes on our behalf. Look at verse 26: "Likewise the Spirit helps us in our weakness; for we do not know how to pray as we ought, but that very Spirit intercedes with sighs too deep for words." We don't even know what to pray for. So the Holy Spirit prays for us, with sighs too deep for words. The Spirit intercedes for us according to the will of the Father; it is the Father's will that the Spirit states our case. What a marvelous privilege it is to have the Holy Spirit pleading on our behalf before the throne of heaven!

So Paul sees only two ways to live—in the flesh or in the Holy Spirit. One is a life without God and the other is a life with all the resources of God. The problem is that most of us Christians have known very well how it feels to have a mixture of the two within us. Most of us have tried to live part of our lives—perhaps most of our lives—in a kind of spiritually comatose state. There has not been a clear separation between "flesh" and Spirit. We have been neither fully alive nor dead.

If we are to stand before God, our hearts must be cleansed of this double-mindedness. God must make us holy so that we will be wholly his. There can be no divided loyalties in the kingdom of God. If you read the biographies of great Christian leaders, you will find how this battle has been fought in their lives.

I remember reading the story of Albert Orsburn, one of the early leaders of the Salvation Army. Orsburn was the great poet and hymn writer of the Salvation Army. In his early ministry, he had been made commander over a district in the city of London. He had an excellent district, and God began to work profoundly among his soldiers. Revival began to break out in the different segments of the Army under his control. Sinners were converted and numbers were being added to their group. Then one day, one of his officers came to him and said, "I have heard a rumor that the brass are going to divide our district." The officer said, "We can't let this happen. God is blessing us so much. If they divide our district, it will hinder the work of God. I think you ought to fight it."

"Oh, no," Orsburn said. "I want to do the will of God and respect my superiors. I will not do that."

Soon his superiors called him in and told him that they indeed planned to divide his district. He said he suddenly found an attitude in his heart that he didn't want. He knew that if they divided that district, his position would not be as prestigious as it was at present. He would not have as much power as before. So he began to argue with his superiors. Looking back on it later, he said, "Unwittingly, I had begun to fight, not for the Kingdom, but for my position in the Kingdom. And the Holy Spirit was grieved."

I will never forget the tone in Orsburn's voice as he told this story. He said, "When the Spirit grieves, the Spirit leaves."

He was a Salvation Army officer, so he managed to keep going through the motions; yet there was a strange distance between Orsburn and God now. A coldness began to move over his spirit. An indifference and a hardness of spirit came. He kept on doing the same thing, but he knew there was an emptiness inside.

Then he was in an automobile accident. He said, "I ended up in the hospital and was a long time in recovery. The gracious Holy Spirit began to deal with my heart once again. One day I heard some singing next door. As I heard them sing of the glories of God, my heart began to yearn again to have that kind of intimacy with God. I wept my heart out in repentance. God forgave me, and the Spirit came and filled my heart afresh."

As a result, Orsburn sat down and wrote a new hymn. He wrote:

*Savior, if my feet have faltered*
*    on the pathway of the Cross,*
*If my purposes have altered*
*    or my gold be mixed with dross,*
*O forbid me not Thy service,*
*    keep me yet in Thy employ,*
*Pass me through a sterner cleansing*
*    if I may but give Thee joy!*[2]

Here was a man who had known God and did not want to lose him; but he knew there was something in his heart separating him from God. Now in penitence he said, "Lord, can you take this rebellious attitude out of me, so that there is an unbroken relationship and I can once again live in the Spirit?"

## WHY THE HOSTILITY?

Why is the Holy Spirit so hostile to what the Scripture calls "the flesh"? Because the flesh is never profitable for anything eternal.

I want to tell you a story that was told to me by an old American preacher, who was giving a series of lectures at Asbury Seminary when I was a student there. One day I was his host and found myself sitting and talking with him. He spoke to me about the man who had been the founder of Asbury Theological Seminary, Henry Clay Morrison. Morrison was one of the greatest preachers in America.

My guest said that he and Morrison once were preaching together in a camp meeting. On Sunday morning, my friend had to preach. A twinkle came to his eye as he said, "Son, there are days when a man preaches better than he is capable of preaching. That day the Holy Spirit descended on me and we had an incredible service. There was a glorious response of sinners seeking God. That night, Dr. Morrison began preaching on Moses' giving the law on Mt.

Sinai. Morrison was a great orator. But the longer he preached the more a little suspicion began to grow inside me. I thought, *We had a great service this morning. Morrison is not used to being with anyone who preaches better than he does. So he thinks that tonight we must have a greater service."*

Finally, the service ended and everyone went to their tents. My guest crawled into his cot and the lights began to go out on the campground. The sounds stopped and everything was very still. Suddenly, my friend heard something rustling in the grass outside his tent. He realized that someone was pulling back the opening of his tent and coming inside. He wondered who it was. The intruder stumbled around until he found the foot of his bed. He knelt in the foot of the preacher's bed, buried his face in the covers over his feet, and began to sob as if his heart would break. He suddenly knew it was the great preacher, Henry Clay Morrison. Neither man said a word. Spirit spoke to spirit.

Then the visiting preacher turned and said to me, "Young man, Henry Clay Morrison was one of the most famous men in the Christian world. But he had gotten into the flesh and he had preached for the sake of his own appearances rather than the glory of God. The Holy Spirit quickened his conscience and convicted him of the sin of it. He could not sleep until he had found his friend and acknowledged his sin."

**THERE IS POWER WHEN WE LIVE IN THE SPIRIT.**

I'm glad Henry Clay Morrison had that kind of sensitivity to the Holy Spirit, because I found Christ as a result of the ministry of that man. My wife also found Christ under the ministry of Henry Clay Morrison.

There is power when we live in the Spirit. There are only sterility and death in the works of the flesh.

The Body of Christ has never learned that. We still squabble for position. We fight for power. We want what we want, when we want it. We try to sanctify our desires by saying, "This is for God." But our motives are mixed. We have a double mind. As a result, our works are sterile. Oh, how we need to have the mind of Christ! Only when we have his mind and live his way can the fullness of the Spirit of God flow through us and be manifest in our living and in our service.

You may think that the phrase "carnal mind" is a bit old-fashioned. Perhaps it is. But it is thoroughly biblical. Whether we use the term or not, we certainly need to understand the truth that Scripture sets before us when it speaks of the "carnal mind." Nowhere is that more obvious than in Romans 8.

Take another look at what Paul says: "For those who live according to the flesh set their minds (Greek, *phroneō*) on the things of the flesh, but those who live according to the Spirit set their minds on the things of the Spirit" (v. 5). There again is that flag word, *phroneō.* Remember that it speaks of a person's entire perspective on life—what one thinks, feels, and aspires to do. Paul is saying that a carnally-minded person is driven by physical desires. The appetites rule. Such a person seeks whatever brings pleasure, whatever "feels good."

In contrast to that is the person who thinks with the mind of Christ. This person has the perspective of Christ's own Spirit. This person seeks whatever pleases the Spirit of the Lord. This person yearns to know where Christ's Spirit is at work and join in that work. The person who sets his mind on the Spirit of Christ sees the world through Christ's eyes and seeks to be a part of what he is doing in the world.

John Wesley referred to this way of thinking as "Christian perfection." Notice what he says in his journal entry for January 27, 1767:

> By perfection, I mean the humble, gentle, patient love of God, and our neighbor, ruling our tempers, words, and actions. I do not include an impossibility of falling from it, either in part or in whole. Therefore, I retract several expressions in our Hymns, which partly express, partly imply, such an impossibility. . . . I believe this perfection is always wrought in the soul by a simple act of faith; consequently, in an instant. But I believe [there is] a gradual work, both preceding and following that instant. . . . As to the time[,] I believe this instant generally is the instant of death, the moment before the soul leaves the body. But I believe it may be ten, twenty, or forty years before. I believe it is usually many years after justification, but it might be within five years or five months after it; I know of no conclusive argument to the contrary.[3]

It's unfortunate that so many people have a distorted view of what Wesley meant by "perfection." He makes it clear that he is talking about the same thing that Paul describes in Romans 8. This is not an experience for a spiritual elite corps; it is God's gift for all of his children. It is a gift that we may not receive till long after our conversion. Indeed, some of us don't receive it until the moment of death. But that doesn't change the fact that life in the Spirit is offered to all of God's people. None of us need to serve our human passions. "We are debtors, not to the flesh, to live according to the flesh" (Romans 8:12), but rather to serve God in the Spirit of his Son, Jesus Christ.

## "MY FATHER IS SO PLEASED"

I met a very winsome young man from Latin America. His father was a professional man. The young man became a Christian at about the age of twenty. He became a very passionate follower of Christ. Within a year after his conversion, he led about sixty other young persons to Christ. I asked him what his ambition was. He said, "My ambition is to be a pastor in Latin America."

At that time, the evangelical church in Latin America was not well respected and not many young people wanted to be evangelical pastors there. When this young man told his father that he planned to be the pastor of a church, his father was horrified. But the young man said, "God has saved me. I want to serve him. I want to be pastor of a church, regardless of the social status it brings."

He came to the United States to get a Christian education. I met him a year or two after he arrived at an evangelical Christian college. I asked, "How is your work going?"

"Oh," he said, "now I am majoring in psychology. I am training to be a psychiatrist and a counselor. My father is so pleased!" This young man, who at one stage was listening to the call of Christ, now for appearances' sake was conforming to the patterns of his unbelieving father and family.

> **PAUL SAYS WE NEED TO STAND UP AGAINST THE STANDARDS OF OUR WORLDLY CULTURE.**

So many of us allow our conduct to be affected by the world around us. We try to please the Lord and please the world at the same time, but Paul says that's impossible.

Paul says we need to stand up against the standards of our worldly culture. We must oppose even the value systems of many of our fellow Christians. We must put ourselves in the places where people need to be touched by Jesus Christ. That means we must go into some very unsavory places, for that is where people need him the most.

God is looking for people who will keep traveling down "the Roman road" from salvation to live as Christ lives. That kind of life takes more than courage. It takes more than insight. It takes the very Spirit of Christ, living within us and animating our lives every day.

---

1. All Scripture references in this chapter are from the *New Revised Standard Version* (NRSV) of the Bible.

2. Albert Orsburn, "All My Work Is for the Master," *The Song Book of the Salvation Army* (Verona, N.J.: Salvation Army, 1986), 473.

3. Thomas Jackson, ed., *The Works of Wesley,* Vol. XI (Grand Rapids: Zondervan Publishing House, n.d.), 446.

Entire sanctification

is primarily

the final settlement

of the

sin question.

—Phineas F. Bresee

From *The Quotable Bresee*, Harold Ivan Smith, comp. (Kansas City: Beacon Hill Press of Kansas City, 1983), 54.

# 10

# THE VOCABULARY OF WESLEYANISM
## —THE MEANING BEHIND THE WORDS—

## J. Kenneth Grider

WESLEY'S MOVEMENT ITSELF, and the later outworkings of it in the Holiness Movement, has always been plagued by "nomenclaturitus." Its terminology has often been misunderstood. Sometimes its terms and phrases have been misappropriated. The perfectly good term *Pentecostal,* for example, is now generally applied to tongues-speaking people, narrowing its use considerably.

To clarify the meaning of key concepts of life in the Spirit, we turn, then, to a discussion of the more common terms used to designate Wesleyanism's distinctive teaching.[1]

### 1. Perfection or Christian Perfection

The term *perfection,* or, as often added to by Wesley and others, *Christian perfection,* is one of the many names for the doctrine of entire sanctification. Perfection is a biblical word, certainly. We are exhorted to go on to "perfection" (Heb. 6:1). We are to be "perfect" (Matt. 5:48), the way our Heavenly Father is, perhaps by loving our enemies (Matt. 5:44). There is, of course, much other such reference to our being perfect, such as 1 Cor. 2:6; Phil. 3:15; 2 Tim. 3:17; etc.

Aside from a given possible contextual meaning as in Matt. 5:43-48, to be perfect, in the New Testament sense, is to have attained the maturity[2] of Christian adulthood by being cleansed of Adamic sin. As a metal is perfect when there is no alloy in it, so we believers are "perfect" when our human nature has had cleansed from it that infection of the human nature known as the carnal nature (see Rom. 8; 1 Cor. 3; Gal. 5:17, 24).

God does not make us perfect in our conduct in the sense that it is faultless. Our conduct is perfect only in the sense that our hearts from such conduct issues are perfect—not being motivated by the carnal nature. At the same time, the conduct is often much less than correct, or much less spiritually sensitive, than it ought to be. As Mr. Wesley was forced to explain often, this kind of perfection is consistent with "infirmities" of varying kinds. So, he wrote: "I say again, let this Christian perfection appear in its own shape, and who will fight against it?"[3]

Thus, while *perfection* is a term often used in Scripture, it unfortunately suggests to "outsiders" a life that is perfect in the fullest possible sense.

## 2. Perfect Love

A term similar to *perfection* (and *Christian perfection*) is *perfect love.* In Scripture, it is referred to mostly in 1 John. There we read, "Whoever confesses that Jesus is the Son of God, God abides in him, and he in God" (4:15).[4] This appears to be a reference to the first work of grace—conversion. John then refers to what Wesleyans have come to call entire sanctification when he adds something to this, about being "perfected." He says, "And [in addition to this] we have come to know and have believed the love which God has for us. God is love, and the one who abides in love abides in God, and God abides in him" (1 John 4:16). John continues: "By this, love is perfected with us, that we may have confidence in the day of judgment; because as He is, so also are we in this world" (4:17). Then John calls this special kind of love "perfect love." He writes, "There is no fear in love; but perfect love casts out fear, because fear involves punishment, and the one who fears is not perfected in love" (4:18).

It is passages such as this that caused Wesley to refer to 1 John more than to any other New Testament book in his *Plain Account of Christian Perfection.* Wesleyans in general, also, have at least found rich entire sanctification teachings in 1 John—although not, in general, to the extent that Wesley did.

However, the term *perfect love,* although used by the apostle John, is misleading to many people who suppose that we mean that our expressions of love to God and others are absolutely flawless. We only mean, however, that such love is not mixed with carnal motivations.

## 3. The Second Blessing

Another term is the *second blessing.* It underscores the fact that entire sanctification is indeed received subsequent to the time of our conversion. It is a special kind of "blessing." Some have incorrectly thought that the term finds scriptural support in 2 Cor. 1:15. J. A. Wood, in the 1880 edition of his book *Perfect Love,* wrote, quoting the KJV:

> The apostle also teaches that "second grace" in 2 Corinthians 1:15: "And in this confidence I was minded to come unto you before that you might have a second benefit" (margin, "second grace"). The original word, *"Barin"* [he means *Charin* from the Greek] here translated "benefit," is translated grace 131 times in the New Testament, and is never rendered "benefit," only in this single instance, and then is corrected by inserting "grace" in the margin.[5]

In the same era of the Holiness Movement Beverly Carradine added to this kind of exegesis. He wrote:

> If King James' translators had been truer to the original in 2 Corinthians 1:15, we would have today the words "second grace" instead of "second benefit." The Greek word translated "benefit" is *charis*. If any Greek scholar should be asked what this word meant in the original, he would never reply "benefit," but "grace," "divine grace," "divine gift," etc.[6]

John Barker, the British Methodist evangelist of recent times, in his *This Is the Will of God,* takes the same kind of view, as have others between Carradine and Barker.[7]

It is correct that the word *charin,* found here, from *charis,* is almost always translated "grace," yet it must be admitted that such a translation here would not fit the context. The context clearly suggests that Paul is talking about a second benefit, or blessing, from his visiting them a second time. The NASB makes the matter clear:

> In this confidence I intended at first to come to you, that you might twice receive a blessing; that is, to pass your way into Macedonia, and again from Macedonia to come to you, and by you to be helped on my journey to Judea (*2 Cor. 1:15-16*).

The NIV makes it even more clear:

> Because I was confident of this [of their appreciation of him], I planned to visit you first so that you might benefit twice. I planned to visit you on my way to Macedonia and to come back to you from Macedonia, and then to have you send me on my way [with a good offering] to Judea (*2 Cor. 1:15-16*).

Besides its being an evident reference to a second benefit to them from a further visit of the apostle, the next paragraph suggests that, at least largely, the people were already in the grace of entire sanctification. He says, "Now He who establishes us with you in Christ and anointed us is God . . . who also sealed us and gave us the Spirit in our hearts as a pledge" (2 Cor. 1:21-22). They had already been "sealed," which is a concomitant of the second work of grace (see Eph. 1:13).

Because some have tried to get holiness "mileage" out of the "second benefit" reference in 2 Cor. 1:15, the term "second blessing" has had about it a certain question. In fact some opponents of second blessing holiness have liked to say that they, too, have received a second blessing, and a third, and a fourth, and so on. Beverly Carradine's response to such comment was that he, too, had received many blessings—but that he had received a thousand or so of those blessings before he had received the second blessing.[8]

## 4. The Second Work of Grace

Very similar to the *second blessing* is the designation *second work of grace.* This is a much more appropriate term, for it has the advantage of being more general.

It includes all the concomitants of holiness doctrine, such as the baptism with the Holy Spirit, cleansing from original sin, empowerment, and sealing.

Unfortunately, Pentecostals in general also believe in a second work of grace in which they, as believers, are "baptized in the Holy Spirit" and speak in tongues. In this connection, Frederick Dale Bruner writes,

> It appears that majority Pentecostalism absorbed from its Methodist parentage the convictions of the subsequent and instantaneous experience and transferred them bodily from Wesley's sanctification to their baptism in the Holy Spirit. In any case, both Methodism and Pentecostalism put their emphasis theologically someplace after justification.[9]

The difference is that Pentecostalism does not include cleansing from original sin but rather tongues-speaking.

## 5. Christian Holiness

A very appropriate name for the doctrine of entire sanctification is *Christian holiness.* The cover of the *Preacher's Magazine,* for a long time, has used this term in its motto: "Proclaiming Christian Holiness."

One advantage of the term is that it is not offensive to outsiders.[10] Lutherans, Mennonites, Calvinists, Presbyterians, Anglicans—even Roman Catholics—all teach, and even emphasize, Christian holiness of some sort. But, though it does not turn people off, neither does it "turn them on." It is vague and broad, with few specifics. It's a ballpark the size of the Pacific Ocean.

## 6. Holiness

The name *holiness* is widely used of Wesleyan Christians and has been for over a century. The Wesleyans have been known as the "holiness people," and the Wesleyan denominations have been known as holiness churches. That movement which started around 1835, and gathered much momentum in the 1860s and beyond, has been known as the Holiness Movement.

But for all that, it is still not precise in meaning. All denominations believe in holiness in some sense, though they would not espouse the doctrine of entire sanctification. Even the Wesleyans often mean something much broader by *holiness* than they do by *entire sanctification.* In popular usage, the two are synonymous; but technically, holiness is begun in the first work of grace (or even in prevenient grace) and it continues, as growth in grace, after entire sanctification.

## 7. Scriptural Holiness

When entire sanctification is called *scriptural holiness,* the meaning is not much sharper. The addition of the adjective *scriptural* helps to underscore the principal source of the doctrine and advertises that the person is a loyal, "true believer," fully orthodox kind of holiness person.

## 8. Second Blessing Holiness

Of all the terms with *holiness* in them, this is perhaps the most definitive. It suggests that this grace is received subsequent to the first work of grace. It defines *holiness* in such a way that it could only describe the Wesleyan tradition and no other. It would exclude the Pentecostal teaching, in which, as we have seen, there is also a second work of grace, because Pentecostals do not refer to this work of grace as holiness. It would exclude what Roman Catholics (and others) would mean by *holiness,* since it is called a "second blessing" kind.

This is not what one would consider a scholarly term. It is a "true believer" kind of designation, often used in personal testimony.

## 9. Our "Canaan"

The use of *Canaan,* or the *Canaan Land experience* (*Beulah* or *Beulah Land* being simply synonyms), as a designation for entire sanctification is a poetic adaptation of an event mentioned often in Scripture (see Heb. 2—4). According to this symbolism, the deliverance of the Israelites from their Egyptian slavery typifies our deliverance from bondage to sin and Satan at our conversion; and crossing over the Jordan river and entering into the land of Canaan typifies entering into the experience of entire sanctification. The analogies have about them a certain plausibility too. Being delivered from Egyptian bondage is indeed analogous to being delivered from a cruel taskmaster who is Satan.

After having had a marvelous deliverance from their bondage to Egypt's Pharaoh, Israel was finally led across the Jordan and given a land that "flowed with milk and honey." This was giving something positive to the delivered people, and even so, those delivered from sin's slavery in conversion are indeed given, positively, an inheritance—in entire sanctification. They are enabled to live a holy life.

The problem here is that there is nothing very exegetically compelling about such an interpretation. One must sort of "reach for it" to interpret it this way and so it is not very convincing to someone not yet convinced about two works of grace. Indeed, many interpret Israel's entering into Canaan much differently. Calvinistic evangelicals view Israel's crossing over the Jordan river as a type of physical death. To them, Canaan, or Beulah, where milk and honey flows, is heaven.

## 10. Wesleyanism

As with so many other designations for entire sanctification, to call it *Wesleyanism* has both advantages and disadvantages. The special advantage is to have one's beliefs associated with a person who is almost comparable to Martin Luther in significance. Abraham Lincoln is perhaps best known as believing that the American union should be preserved, so for one of that day to say that he was a "Lincolnite" would be widely understood. He would be associating himself with the well-known philosophy of a popular figure. Something like that is involved when we holiness people call ourselves "Wesleyans."

And a person does not need to agree with his spiritual forebear in all respects in order to associate himself with that figure. Calvinists, for example, might differ with John Calvin on some aspect of the doctrine of absolute sovereignty and still properly be called Calvinists. So those in the Holiness Movement may properly call themselves Wesleyans, even though, on entire sanctification, they would probably not hold identical positions with Wesley, particularly at the point of its relationship to the baptism with the Holy Spirit.

## 11. The Baptism with the Holy Spirit

This term is, by and large, an American addition to John Wesley's teachings. In our using it, we declare our belief that this is the way in which entire sanctification happens. The term is roughly biblical, and within the Holiness Movement has long been associated with the doctrine of entire sanctification.

The chief disadvantage in using the term is that the Pentecostals and neo-Pentecostals use only a slightly different phrase, "the baptism *in* the Holy Spirit," to mean something quite different. They do not believe that it cleanses from original sin, but incorrectly teach that one receives at the time either an initial evidence in tongues-speaking or a special tongues-speaking gift.

## 12. Heart Purity

Though this designation for entire sanctification is not nearly as widely used as some of the others, it clearly indicates what happens in the experience. What Wesley liked to call "inward sin"—the sin of the heart, out of which, as Jesus said, acts of sin come forth (see Mark 7:23)—is cleansed. Holiness people have been fond of pointing to one of the Beatitudes as support for this teaching where Jesus said, "Blessed are the pure in heart, for they shall see God" (Matt. 5:8).

## 13. The Fullness of the Blessing

This term is similar to *full salvation*—a designation widely used by The Salvation Army, which for some years now has been officially a member of the Christian Holiness Association. The "fullness" thought suggests a positive note.

> WHILE CONSECRATION IS SOMETHING WE DO BY GOD'S HELP, SANCTIFICATION IS SOMETHING GOD DOES FOR US.

Although the term might imply that the first work of grace is somehow only partial, and not complete, in some sense this is true. The scriptural call is to "go unto perfection" (Heb. 6:1, KJV), and perfection suggests a full or complete salvation.

## 14. Sanctification

This term is similar to *holiness*, discussed earlier. It is different, however, in that *holiness*, popularly, has to do in part with what we do in order to live a devout life—the living out of our consecration to God's full will in our lives. While consecration is something we do by God's help, sanctification is something God does for us.

Consecration involves what we purpose to do with our talents, our money, etc. We consecrate them to God, and He sanctifies them in the sense of separating them from common uses to His uses. In this sense, in Old Testament times, the Levitical priesthood was sanctified, as were the Sabbath, tithes, sacrifices, etc.

The term *sanctification* has the advantage of being a word that most people would at least somewhat understand. And Holy Scripture itself often uses *sanctification* as referring to something God does in us. In Eph. 5:25-26, Paul says, "Christ also loved the church and gave Himself up for her; that He might sanctify her, having cleansed her by the washing of water with the Word." Scripture customarily uses *sanctification* instead of *entire sanctification*, only once expressly using what suggests the latter term (1 Thess. 5:23).

## 15. Entire Sanctification

All things considered, *entire sanctification* is perhaps the most preferable designation for Wesleyanism's distinctive emphasis.[11] Among the points in its favor are: (1) it is widely used and widely understood; (2) John Wesley himself used it quite frequently and urged its use, establishing thereby a tradition within Methodism and the Holiness Movement generally; and (3) it suggests the doctrine's most significant aspect: the cleansing away of original sin. This experience of entire sanctification is wrought by, or effected by, or occasioned by the baptism with the Holy Spirit.[12]

---

1. Editor's note: For additional insight regarding the vocabulary of holiness, see J. B. Chapman's book *The Terminology of Holiness* (Kansas City: Beacon Hill Press of Kansas City, 1968).

2. Note RSV's translation as "mature," e.g., Phil. 3:15. And note that H. Orton Wiley, in his *Epistle to the Hebrews,* 202, suggests that the *hoi teleioi,* the perfect ones, are mature persons—not in the sense of spiritual richness that comes with growth, but in the sense that at age 21 a person is mature in the sense of attaining to his full adulthood (Kansas City: Beacon Hill Press, 1953).

3. John Wesley, *A Plain Account of Christian Perfection,* reprint ed. (Kansas City: Beacon Hill Press of Kansas City, 1966), 107.

4. Unless otherwise indicated, all Scripture references in this chapter are from the *New American Standard Bible* (NASB).

5. John Allen Wood, *Perfect Love,* rev. ed. (South Pasadena, Calif.: John A. Wood, 1894), 197.

6. Wood had said 131 times. They are both talking about *charis* in its various forms.

7. John Barker, *This Is the Will of God* (London: Epworth Press, 1954), 52.

8. See Beverly Carradine, *The Second Blessing in Symbol* (Louisville, Ky.: Pickett Publishing Co., 1896), 17-18.

9. Frederick Dale Bruner, *A Theology of the Holy Spirit* (Grand Rapids: Wm. B. Eerdmans, 1970), 38.

10. A similar inoffensive term—even beguiling—is in Hannah Whitall Smith, *The Christian's Secret of a Happy Life* (Westwood, N.J.: Fleming H. Revell, n.d.). More than 3,000,000 copies of this book have been sold, making it by far the most widely used of all holiness books. Indeed, until recent years, it enjoyed one of the widest circulations of any book—second to the *Pilgrim's Progress* and Charles Sheldon's *In His Steps,* but not to many others. Probably the other most widely circulated holiness book is Chester Arthur's *Tongue of Fire,* which was published in at least 12 languages. Neither Hannah Smith's book nor Arthur's, however, are very definitively or specifically or expressly on entire sanctification. That is the chief doctrine which these authors are elucidating in these books. But they do so in disguised ways—this being somewhat more so in Hannah Smith's classic. You have to search all through, as a reader, to be confident that the Christian's secret of a happy life is to receive sanctification.

11. The books with "entire sanctification" in the title are: S. L. C. Coward, *Entire Sanctification* (Chicago: Christian Witness Co., 1928); John Hunt, *Entire Sanctification: Its Nature, the Way of Its Attainment, Motives for Its Pursuit* (London: John Mason, 1860); W. Jones, *The Doctrine of Entire Sanctification* (Philadelphia: National Association for the Promotion of Holiness, 1885); Paul Kindschi, *Entire Sanctification* (Marion, Ind.: Wesley Press, 1964); C. W. Ruth, *Entire Sanctification* (Chicago: Christian Witness Co., 1903); C. B. Whitaker, *Entire Sanctification: A Second Work of Grace* (Grand Rapids: S. B. Shaw, Holiness Record Office, 1887); A. Zepp, *Progress After Entire Sanctification* (Chicago: Christian Witness Co., 1909).

12. See *Manual, Church of the Nazarene* (Kansas City: Nazarene Publishing House, 1976), articles V and X of the Articles of Faith.

Originally published as "The Nomenclature of Wesleyanism," chapter 3 of *Entire Sanctification: The Distinctive Doctrine of Wesleyanism* (Kansas City: Nazarene Publishing House, 1980), 34-43.

Men are unhappy because

they are unholy.

Pain accompanies

and follows sin.

Why is the earth so full

of complicated distress?

Because it is full

of complicated wickedness.

It is impossible,

in the nature of things,

that wickedness

can consist

with happiness.

—John Wesley

From *Through the Year with Wesley,* Frederick Hill, ed. (Nashville: The Upper Room, 1983), 156.

# 11

# A PRAYER FOR ENTIRE SANCTIFICATION
## —"May He Strengthen Your Heart in Holiness"—

## William M. Greathouse

IN EXAMINING THE FOUNDATIONS for the holy life, no book is more important than 1 Thessalonians. Regarded by many scholars as the earliest of Paul's letters (about A.D. 50), it is therefore the oldest piece of Christian literature in existence.

Most significantly, 1 Thessalonians contains a higher density of specific holiness terms than any other Pauline letter, with a percentage twice the average of the entire body of his letters. Paul's benedictory prayer in 5:23-24, the only explicit reference to *entire* sanctification in his writings, summarizes the apostle's concerns in the letter and witnesses to the centrality of holiness in 1 Thessalonians.[1]

As a young Christian, I read the five brief chapters of 1 Thessalonians in one sitting for my evening devotions. That evening I found a narrative account of Christian holiness that squared with what I had been taught as a new Nazarene, an understanding that has been a lodestar in my theology ever since.

Try it for yourself. Before reading further in this chapter, please consult 1 Thessalonians for yourself. Take a few minutes and read the five short chapters; then with your Bible open before you, consider the outline that follows "to see whether these things [are] so" (Acts 17:11).[2]

## THE THESSALONIANS WERE TRUE BELIEVERS (1:1—2:16)

Everything Paul says about his Thessalonian converts witnesses to their genuine conversion to Christianity. They beautifully exemplified faith, hope, and love, evidence of their true Christian experience (1:3): "a moral life marked by faithfulness to God, hopeful expectation of final salvation, and fraternal love in the meantime."[3]

The Thessalonians' salvation was clearly demonstrated. The gospel had come to them "not in word only, but also in power and in the Holy Spirit and with full conviction" (vv. 4-5). "In spite of persecution" they had "received the word with joy inspired by the Holy Spirit," thereby becoming "an example to all the believers" of the region (vv. 6-7). They had "turned to God from idols, to serve a living and true God, and to wait for his Son from heaven" (vv. 9-10).

The second chapter continues the story of their faith and of the loving relationship that existed between them and the apostle. It likens the Thessalonian church to "the churches of God in Christ Jesus . . . in Judea," in that these believers had "suffered the same things from [their] own compatriots" that the churches in Judea had suffered from "the Jews, who killed both the Lord Jesus and the prophets" (2:14-15).

## THE THESSALONIANS' FAITH HAD STOOD THE TEST OF SEVERE PERSECUTION (2:17—3:9)

Paul's preaching at Thessalonica had stirred up unbelieving Jews who "formed a mob and set the city in an uproar. . . . That very night the believers sent Paul and Silas off to Beroea" (Acts 17:5, 10; see vv. 1-10). In this way Paul was forced to leave—"in person, not in heart" (1 Thess. 2:17)—the newly converted pagans in Thessalonica. "We longed with great eagerness to see you face to face," Paul writes, "But Satan blocked our way. For what is our hope or joy or crown of boasting before our Lord Jesus at his coming? Is it not you? Yes, you are our glory and joy!" (vv. 17-20).

When he could bear it no longer, Paul dispatched Timothy from Athens (where he had gone from Berea) to "strengthen and encourage" (3:2) the Thessalonians, lest they be "shaken by these persecutions" (v. 3), and his labor among them be proven to have "been in vain" (v. 5).

"But Timothy has just now come to us from you," Paul continues, "and has brought us the good news of your faith and love. . . . For we now live, if you continue to stand firm in the Lord" (vv. 6, 8). The encouraging report gave the apostle an occasion of rejoicing before God (vv. 6, 8-9).

## THE THESSALONIANS HAD A REMAINING LACK IN FAITH (3:10—4:12)

Despite their triumphant endurance and evident love, we now read, Paul was "night and day praying exceedingly" for the Thessalonians, "that [he] may see [them] and *perfect* [supply—NIV, RSV] what [was] lacking in [their] faith" (3:10, NKJV, emphasis added). The Greek verb in the latter clause comes from a root that means "rendering complete," "fitting together," or "reconciling factions." It is used here to mean the supplying of what is missing for the full discharge of the functions for which these believers were designed of God (cf. Eph. 4:12).[4]

Paul's prayer to see the Thessalonians "face to face" has theological significance. The apostolic presence is commonly linked with the desire to perfect a church's faith (cf. Rom. 1:11).[5] Having been abruptly removed from Thessalonica, the apostle now longs to return *in person* and *perfect* their inadequate faith and experience.

The imperfection of the Thessalonians was in two interrelated areas: in their *love* and in their *holiness* (3:11—4:12). Both were genuine, but their love needed to be perfected and their holiness completed.

In addressing these remaining deficiencies, the apostle's approach is noticeably positive. His attitude is clearly revealed in his prayer for the church:

> Now may our God and Father himself and our Lord Jesus Christ direct our way to you. *And may the Lord make you increase and abound in love* for one another and for all, just as we abound in love for you. *And may he so strengthen your hearts in holiness* that you may be blameless before our God and Father at the coming of our Lord Jesus with all his saints (*3:11-13, emphases added*).

This prayer suggests clearly that abounding love and blamelessness in holiness are two aspects of one whole.

A look at 4:9-12 shows again Paul's positive approach to their need for a fullness of love: "Now concerning love of the brothers and sisters, you do not need to have anyone write to you," he explains, *"for you yourselves have been taught by God to love one another; and indeed you do love. . . .* But we urge you, beloved, *to do so more and more"* (4:9-10, emphases added; see Eph. 3:14-19).

With respect to their holiness, the apostle takes the same approach when he writes, "Finally, brothers and sisters, we ask and urge you in the Lord Jesus that, as you have learned from us how you ought to live and please God (*as, in fact, you are doing), you should do so more and more"* (4:1, emphasis added). Then specific injunctions follow that spell out what it means to be holy in heart and life, in a pagan culture rife with immorality and seething with lustful passion. Lyons explains,

**THE APOSTLE INCARNATED THE GOSPEL HE PREACHED, AND HE EXPECTED HIS CONVERTS TO IMITATE HIM.**

> Paul proceeds from the theological assumption that the character of Christians is fundamentally different from that of pagans because of the character of their God. Pagans behave as they do because they "do not know God" (4:5; cf. 2 Thess. 1:8; Gal. 4:9). Paul characterizes his moral teaching to the Thessalonians as an exhortation to "lead a life worthy of God, who calls you into his own kingdom and glory" (2:12).[6]

"This is the will of God," Paul urges, "your sanctification: that you abstain from unchastity" (4:3, RSV). The apostle's instruction was not "Do as I *say*," but

"Do as I *do*." Earlier in the letter he had reminded them: "You are witnesses, and God also, how pure, upright, and blameless our conduct was toward you believers" (2:10; see 1:5-6; 2:3-4; 2 Cor. 1:12). The apostle *incarnated* the gospel he preached, and he expected his converts to imitate him in leading "a life worthy of God, who calls you into his own kingdom and glory" (2:12)—a life of transparent holiness.[7]

God did not call the Thessalonians "to impurity but in holiness" (4:7). The Greek noun for "holiness" here (*hagiasmos*, as in verses 3 and 7) defines a *process* of sanctification: "a divine activity which is manifest in concrete activity on the part of the faithful."[8] The idea conveyed is that the Thessalonians had been called of God in the *realm* of holiness. Therefore, anyone who rejects the call to *entire* sanctification "rejects not human authority but God, who also gives His Holy Spirit to you," paraphrased by J. B. Phillips, "It is not for nothing that the Spirit God gives us is called the *Holy* Spirit" (v. 8). True holiness is not a human dogma; it is the work of the sanctifying Spirit that we reject at the danger of our own loss. And holiness must embrace the sexual realm of our experience. Although self-idolatry is the *root* of sin, sexual immorality is its first and most obvious *fruit* (see Rom. 1:21-27; Gal. 5:19). The holy life is a life of moral purity.

## THE APOSTLE PRAYS THE THESSALONIANS WILL BE *ENTIRELY* SANCTIFIED

May the God of peace himself sanctify you entirely; and may your spirit and soul and body be kept sound and blameless at the coming of our Lord Jesus Christ. The one who calls you is faithful, and he will do this (5:23-24).

This prayer is clearly "the summit of the epistle." It repeats Paul's "prayer-wish" in 3:9-13 and pulls together all the vital elements of his instructions in 4:1 through 5:22, bringing to a climax the entire Epistle. Within this prayer we see a conscious and deliberate summary of all that has come before, in this comprehensive benediction.[9]

This benedictory prayer is threefold, revealing the *subject*, the *scope*, and the *surety* of entire sanctification.

### The Subject

"The emphasis is on God *himself* as the acting subject," says Spross.[10] While the Holy Spirit is the active Agent in effecting sanctification (see 2 Thess. 2:13), He does not operate without human cooperation, as Paul's exhortations to holy living clearly imply. God's call to holiness can be rejected (see 1 Thess. 4:8). The Spirit purifies, motivates, and enables holy living, but our personal participation is always presupposed.[11] As Augustine and others have said, "Without God we cannot; without us God will not."

> "WITHOUT GOD WE CANNOT; WITHOUT US GOD WILL NOT."

While putting ourselves at God's disposal is essential to true sanctification (see Rom. 6:13, 19), only "the God of peace himself" (1 Thess. 5:23) can accomplish our entire sanctification. For Paul the Jew, the peace God gives is *shalom*, true well-being, wholeness, and blessedness. Here it also means "final salvation, which is the ultimate blessing which the Lord gives to his people."[12]

Paul employs the aorist tense here, a usage that lends itself to the view that sanctification comes to completion within a process that begins at conversion and continues to the return of Christ. One scholar goes so far as to suggest that the verb here "must mean 'conform to the nature of God.' This certainly includes moral perfection without being limited to it."[13] God himself sanctifies us in our consecration, in our total separation from sin, and in our self-abandonment to His working within us. Leon Morris points out that "while there is a human element, in that a man must yield himself up to God (see 4:4), yet the primary thing is the power of God which enables this to be made good."[14]

### The Scope

"May the God of peace himself sanctify you *entirely*" (1 Thess. 5:23, emphasis added). The compound adverb *holoteleis,* found only here in the New Testament, literally means "wholly and perfectly." "Carrying the sense of fullness, completeness, and totality," Dan Spross explains, "the sanctification prayed for is an entire sanctification."[15] The NIV "through and through" follows Luther's German *durch und durch.* Paul's prayer is for the Thessalonians' *total* moral and spiritual renovation, the concern of Charles Wesley's prayer when he wrote,

> *Finish then Thy new creation;*
> *Pure and spotless let us be.*
> *Let us see Thy great salvation,*
> *Perfectly restored in Thee.*

Other scholars find a further implication in the adverb. Leon Morris observes,

> The point is that the word is a compound of which the first part has the meaning "wholly." If the second part is to have its proper significance we need something to bring out the thought of reaching one's proper end, the end for which one was made.[16]

Then we must ask, "What is the proper end for which we were made?" Adam Clarke says to this very point, "As God requires every man to love him with all the heart, soul, mind, and strength, and his neighbour as himself; then he is a perfect man that does so; *he answers to the end for which God made him*" (emphasis added).[17] Entire sanctification is to the end or purpose of perfect love.[18]

Paul's prayer for the Thessalonians' sanctification includes the further petition for their preservation in holiness. "And may your spirit and soul and body be kept sound [or 'complete,' margin] and blameless at the coming of our Lord Jesus Christ" (5:23). The majority of interpreters take the terms "spirit and soul and body" in a collective sense, signifying the totality of the human personality. Even though the apostle is using Greek terms, he is thinking as a Hebrew, like our Lord when He commanded that we love God with all our heart and soul and mind (see Matt. 22:37)—that is, with our entire being. Entire sanctification is moral and spiritual *wholeness,* spiritual health restored and preserved by the power of God.

Thank God, we may be kept "blameless at the coming of our Lord Jesus Christ" (5:23). Blamelessness is not to be taken as something to be reserved for the moment of Christ's appearing. The word translated "kept" *(tērētheiē)* has a double connotation, including not only the idea of conservation and preservation but also the idea of shielding, defending, and protecting. According to Gordon Pitts Wiles, the term "implies the continuation of that which already exists—so their present sanctification will be maintained at the parousia. The prayer that they may be kept wholly blameless at the parousia therefore implies their present sanctification as well."[19] In this vein, Ernest Best writes: "Holiness, of course, will not come suddenly into existence then unless they are now already 'holy' and seeking holiness. If believers are preserved in the Day of Judgment, this will imply preservation until then."[20]

"How much religion must I have?" someone asked. Answer: "Enough to be comfortable at the thought that Christ may come at any moment." The truly sanctified pray with John the revelator, "Amen. Come, Lord Jesus!" (Rev. 22:20).

### The Surety

"The one who calls you is faithful, and he will do this" (1 Thess. 5:24). Like justifying faith, sanctifying faith gives "glory to God; . . . being fully persuaded that, what he had promised, he was able also to perform" (Rom. 4:20-21, KJV).

"But what is that faith whereby we are sanctified—saved from sin and perfected in love?" John Wesley asks. He answers:

It is a divine evidence and conviction, First, that God hath promised it in the Holy Scripture. Till we are thoroughly satisfied of this, there is no moving one step further. And one would imagine there needed not one word more to satisfy a reasonable man of this, than the ancient promise, "Then will I circumcise thy heart, and the heart of thy seed, to love the Lord thy God with all thy heart and with all thy soul . . ." How clearly does this express the being perfected in love!—how strongly imply the being saved from all sin! For as long as love fills up the whole heart what room is there for sin therein?

It is a divine evidence and conviction, Secondly, that what God hath promised He is able to perform. Admitting, therefore, that "with men it is impossible," yet this creates no difficulty in the case, seeing "with God all things are possible." . . . If God speaks, it shall be done . . .

It is, Thirdly, a divine evidence and conviction that He is able and willing to do it now. And why not? Is not a moment to Him the same as a thousand years? He cannot want more time to accomplish whatever is His will. And He cannot want or stay for any more *worthiness* or *fitness* in the persons He is pleased to honour. We may therefore boldly say, at any point of time, "Now is the day of salvation!" "Today, if ye will hear His voice, harden not your hearts!" . . .

To this confidence, that God is both able and willing to sanctify us now, there needs to be added only one thing more, a divine evidence and conviction that He *doeth* it. In that hour it is done. . . . The believer then experiences the deep meaning of those solemn words, "If we walk in the light as He is in the light, we have fellowship one with another, and the blood of Jesus Christ His Son cleanseth from all sin."[21]

While serving as president of Nazarene Theological Seminary in Kansas City, I was invited to meet with ministers of Kirksville, Missouri, to engage in an exegesis of Romans, chapters 6 through 8. Fifteen or 16 ministers representing major denominations were present, along with the Roman Catholic priest and the Nazarene and Assembly of God pastors. We met at a small white country church outside the city. Sitting around a large table, we worked through chapters 6 and 7 before lunch. After lunch we spent more than an hour in chapter 8. I was deeply impressed by the unity of understanding that seemed to prevail as we simply endeavored to let the apostle speak to us from this Epistle. By midafternoon we had come to the definitive statement of the chapter: "Those who are in the flesh cannot please God. But you are not in the flesh, you are in the Spirit, if in fact the Spirit of God [really] dwells in you" (vv. 8-9, RSV, emphasis added). I emphasized that when Paul wrote, "You are not in the flesh, you are in the Spirit," he was not writing to the saints in heaven, but to the saints in Rome.

I then felt led to share my own witness to the Spirit's sanctifying grace. When I concluded, the Baptist pastor, sitting in a cane-bottomed chair next to me, asked, "But how can you *know* when you are truly sanctified?" I was about to respond when the Roman Catholic priest, sitting on a high stool next to his Protestant brother, interrupted. Putting his hand on the latter's bald head, he said kindly, "The day came when, looking into the mirror as you shaved, you said to yourself, 'Why, I'm bald-headed!' So there comes that moment when, yielded to God in full obedience, we exclaim to ourselves, 'It's done!'"

"But how do you know that you are sanctified, saved from your inbred corruption?" Wesley asks. He

> **ENTIRE SANCTIFICATION IS A LIFE-CHANGING WORK OF GOD'S GRACE THAT PURIFIES THE HEART FROM ITS SELF-IDOLATRY.**

answers, "We know it by the witness and by the fruit of the Spirit."[22] The fruit corroborates the witness. Entire sanctification is more than an experience; it is a life-changing work of God's grace that purifies the heart from its self-idolatry, perfects it in the love of God and neighbor, and accelerates the believer's growth in Christlikeness. As it was God's promise to entirely sanctify the Thessalonians, it is also His promise to do this for us today! *"The one who called you is faithful, and He will do this"* (1 Thess. 5:24, emphasis added).

> *O for a heart to praise my God,*
> *A heart from sin set free,*
> *A heart that always feels Thy blood*
> *So freely shed for me.*
>
> *A heart resigned, submissive, meek,*
> *My great Redeemer's throne,*
> *Where only Christ is heard to speak,*
> *Where Jesus reigns alone.*
>
> *O for a lowly contrite heart,*
> *Believing, true, and clean,*
> *Which neither life nor death can part*
> *From Him that dwells within.*
>
> *A heart in ev'ry thought renewed*
> *And full of love divine,*
> *Perfect and right and pure and good—*
> *A copy, Lord, of Thine.*
>
> —Charles Wesley

---

1. George Lyons, "Modeling the Holiness Ethos: A Study Based on First Thessalonians," *Wesleyan Theological Journal* 30, No. 1 (spring 1995): 188-89.

2. Unless otherwise indicated, all Scripture references in this chapter are from the *New Revised Standard Version* of the Bible.

3. Lyons, "Modeling the Holiness Ethos," 194.

4. Daniel Brett Spross, "Sanctification in the Thessalonian Epistles in a Canonical Context" (Ph.D. diss., Southern Baptist Theological Seminary, 1987), 21 (citing J. B. Lightfoot). The Greek verb *katartisai* and its derivatives occur in the New Testament with a wide variety of meanings. The disciples were *"mending* their nets" (Matt. 4:21; Mark 1:19; emphasis added). The fractious Corinthians were commanded to *"become perfect"* (2 Cor. 13:9, emphasis added). The NRSV rendering of *katartisai, "restore"* (emphasis added), violates the context; there is no evidence in the Epistle of any loss of faith on the part of the Thessalonians.

5. Suggested in private conversation by Alex R. G. Deasley.

6. Lyons, "Modeling the Holiness Ethos," 191-92.

7. The adverb translated "worthy" does not imply that moral living is a means of earning God's call to Kingdom glory. Rather, it is "a recognition that God's call to future salvation makes certain behaviors 'appropriate' in the present. A Holy God demands a holy people (cf. 1 Pet. 1:13-16)" (Lyons, 203).

8. Spross, "Sanctification in the Thessalonian Epistles," 34.

9. Ibid., 41-42.

10. Ibid., 43.

11. Lyons, "Modeling the Holiness Ethos," 192. The clearest illustration of this necessary human cooperation in order to effect sanctification is Paul's injunction in Rom. 6:12-19.

12. Spross, "Sanctification in the Thessalonian Epistles," 44, quoting Ernest Best, *A Commentary on the First and Second Epistles to the Thessalonians* (New York: Harper and Row, 1972), 242.

13. Spross, "Sanctification in the Thessalonian Epistles," 46, quoting D. E. H. Whiteley, *The Theology of St. Paul* (London: Oxford University Press, 1964), 85.

14. Leon Morris, "The First and Second Epistles to the Thessalonians," in *The New International Commentary on the New Testament* (Grand Rapids: William B. Eerdmans Publishing Co., 1959), 180.

15. Spross, "Sanctification in the Thessalonian Epistles," 46.

16. Morris, "First and Second Epistles to the Thessalonians," 80. The second half of the adverb, *teleis*, derives from the root *telos*, meaning "end," "goal," "purpose." D. Edmond Hiebert explains *holoteleis*: "wholly affecting the end, reaching the intended goal, hence has here the force of no part being left untouched" (*A Call to Readiness: The Thessalonian Epistles* [Chicago: Moody Press, 1971], 251).

17. Adam Clarke, *Christian Theology*, ed. Samuel Dunn (New York: T. Mason and G. Lane, 1840), 183.

18. Thus, John Wesley uses "entire sanctification" and "Christian perfection" interchangeably.

19. Spross, "Sanctification in the Thessalonian Epistles," 50, quoting Gordon Pitts Wiles, "The Function of Intercessory Prayer in Paul's Apostolic Ministry with Special Reference to the First Epistle to the Thessalonians" (Ph.D. diss., Yale University, 1965), 132.

20. Spross, "Sanctification in the Thessalonian Epistles," 51, quoting Best, *A Commentary*, 182.

21. John Wesley, "The Scripture Way of Salvation," in *Wesley's Standard Sermons*, ed. Edward H. Sugden (London: Epworth Press, 1921) 2:257-59.

22. John Wesley, *A Plain Account of Christian Perfection* (Kansas City: Beacon Hill Press of Kansas City, 1966), 86.

Originally published as chapter 8 of *Love Made Perfect: Foundations for the Holy Life* (Kansas City: Beacon Hill Press of Kansas City, 1997), 86-100.

# CONTRIBUTORS TO
# *A HOLY PASSION*

## J. B. CHAPMAN

Dr. J. B. Chapman started his ministry as an evangelist at age 16 and pastored churches in Oklahoma, Texas, and Arkansas. In the course of his influential ministry, he served as district superintendent, college president, founding editor of *Preacher's Magazine,* editor of *Herald of Holiness,* and general superintendent. His message "All Out for Souls" to the district superintendents in 1946 focused the Church of the Nazarene away from introspective legalism to outward mission and achievement. As one of the second-generation leaders in Nazarene history, he helped shape the denomination's future with the many facets of his ministry of preaching, administration, and writing.

## H. RAY DUNNING

Dr. H. Ray Dunning served as professor of theology at Trevecca Nazarene College (now University) for nearly 30 years. Prior to teaching, he pastored Nazarene congregations for 20 years throughout Tennessee and in Arkansas. He has authored, edited, and contributed to numerous books on Christian theology, faith, and practice, including *Grace, Faith, and Holiness; The Second Coming; A Layman's Guide to Sanctification;* and *Biblical Resources for Holiness Preaching* (Volumes 1 and 2). Dr. Dunning retired in 1995 from Trevecca but continues to teach, preach, and write.

## WILLIAM M. GREATHOUSE

Dr. William M. Greathouse served as general superintendent from 1976 until 1989. Previous ministry assignments include 8 years as president of Nazarene Theological Seminary, president of Trevecca Nazarene College (now University) in Nashville, and pastoral service to Nazarene congregations for 23 years. His fruitful writing ministry includes *The Fullness of the Spirit, From the Apostles to Wesley, Love Made Perfect, Wholeness in Christ,* and as coauthor *Introduction to Wesleyan Theology* and *Exploring Christian Holiness* (Vol. II). In 1997, the Wesleyan Theological Society honored him with the "Lifetime Service to the Wesleyan/Holiness Tradition" award. Dr. Greathouse resides in the Nashville area and continues to teach and preach.

## J. KENNETH GRIDER

Dr. J. Kenneth Grider taught theology at Nazarene Theological Seminary for nearly 50 years. He is well known for his prolific writing. Grider has authored innumerable articles and books, including *Entire Sanctification, A Wesleyan-Holiness Theology,* and *Isaiah—Daniel* (Vol. 4 of the *Beacon Bible Commentary*). He also served as consulting editor for the *Beacon Dictionary of Theology.* Dr. Grider lives in retirement in Arizona and Kansas City.

## ALBERT F. HARPER

Dr. Albert F. Harper served every Nazarene for more than a quarter of a century as editor-in-chief of all Sunday School materials and as executive director of the Church Schools

Division at Nazarene Headquarters. During his tenure as denominational Sunday School executive, he started more than 20 new curriculum pieces, wrote 13 weeks of adult curriculum materials every year, and edited every word of every lesson of every age-group during that period. He was a prolific writer and is well known for the Beacon Hill Press classic, *Holiness and High Country*. He has also written a number of books, including *Now That Retirement Has Come, The Story of Ourselves, Great Holiness Classics* Vol. 6, and *Exploring Christian Education*. He edited the *Wesley Study Bible* and the five-volume *Holiness Classics Series*. Dr. Harper taught at Nazarene Theological Seminary, Eastern Nazarene College, and Northwest Nazarene College (now University). He taught a well-attended adult Sunday School class until his 90th birthday.

## DENNIS F. KINLAW

Dr. Dennis F. Kinlaw, founder of the Francis Asbury Society and former president of Asbury College, has served Christ and the Church as preacher, Old Testament scholar, and administrator of higher education. In 1963, he joined the faculty of Asbury Theological Seminary as professor of Old Testament. Five years later he was invited to serve as president of Asbury College; he led the college from 1968 to 1981 and again from 1986 to 1991. Dr. Kinlaw has contributed to a number of publications, including commentaries on Ecclesiastes and the Song of Songs in the *Wesleyan Bible Commentary*, and Leviticus in the *Beacon Bible Commentary*. He has written articles for a number of magazines, journals, and anthologies and is the author of several books: *Preaching in the Spirit, The Mind of Christ*, and his recent devotional book, *This Day with the Master*. In retirement he continues an active ministry of preaching and writing.

## FRANK M. MOORE

Dr. Frank M. Moore pastored for five years in Ohio before joining the religion faculty of Trevecca Nazarene University. He moved to MidAmerica Nazarene University in 1985 where he served as chairman of the Division of Religion and Philosophy before accepting his current position as vice president for academic affairs and the academic dean. Dr. Moore continues to teach religion courses and is the author of several books, including *Breaking Free from Sin, Coffee Shop Theology, More Coffee Shop Theology*, and *Dismantling the Myths* and contributed three chapters to *Holiness 101*.

## W. T. PURKISER

Dr. W. T. Purkiser—with his gifted teaching, writing, and preaching—helped systematize and strengthen the theological foundations of the Church of the Nazarene. After pastoring on the Southern California District from 1930 to 1937, he served as professor, dean, vice president, and eventually president of Pasadena College (now Point Loma Nazarene University). Following Purkiser's long service at the college, he was appointed professor of English Bible at Nazarene Theological Seminary. He went on to serve as editor of the *Herald of Holiness* for 14 years. As a faithful churchman, Dr. Purkiser sat on the General Council of the Nazarene Young People's Society and also the Council of Education. In the course of his years of active service, he authored 26 books, among them *God, Man, and Salvation*, a classic theology text still referred to as a cornerstone of Nazarene theology.

# TIMOTHY L. SMITH

No one tracked early Nazarene history better than Dr. Timothy L. Smith. Historian, pastor, teacher, and preacher, he began early, conducting revivals well before he graduated from college at the University of Virginia. Dr. Smith edited, authored, and contributed to dozens of articles, essays, and books. His first book, *Revivalism and Social Reform,* was an award-winning major national publication and has been in print nearly continuously since 1957. He wrote essays on religion, higher education, and the role of ethnicity in shaping American religion and coauthored *The Promise of the Spirit,* a historical biography of Charles G. Finney. He regarded as his most outstanding professional achievement the publication of his second book, *Called unto Holiness* (1962), a history of Nazarene origins and early development. In the course of his long career, Smith also taught American history at Johns Hopkins University and served as president of the American Society of Church History.

# RICHARD S. TAYLOR

Dr. Richard S. Taylor is professor emeritus of theology and missions at Nazarene Theological Seminary where he taught from 1961 to 1977. He taught on the faculty of Eastern Nazarene College before coming to NTS. He served the church as president/rector of overseas missions schools in Australia and Switzerland, as first director of pastoral ministry at Nazarene Headquarters, and as editor of the *Preacher's Magazine.* His distinguished ministry also included pastorates on the New England, Oregon Pacific, and Northwest Districts and six years as an evangelist. Dr. Taylor makes his home in Covina, California, and maintains an active schedule of writing, preaching, and teaching. His significant contributions as an author include *The Disciplined Life; Exploring Christian Holiness, Vol. 3; The Theological Formulation;* and *A Right Conception of Sin.*

# JOHN WESLEY

Evangelist and founder of Methodism, John Wesley was born into a strong Anglican home: his father, Samuel, was a priest, and his mother, Susanna, taught religion and morals faithfully to her 19 children. He studied at Oxford, was ordained deacon (1725) and priest (1728), and in 1726 became a fellow at Oxford and lecturer in Greek. Influenced by the spiritual writings of William Law, he became leader of a small group, nicknamed the Methodists, which had gathered around his brother Charles, a name later adopted by John for the adherents of the great evangelical movement that was its outgrowth. On their father's death, the brothers went as missionaries to Georgia (1735-38), but the mission proved a failure. In 1738, at a meeting in London, during the reading of Luther's preface to the Epistle to the Romans, he experienced an assurance of salvation that convinced him that he must bring the same assurance to others; but his zeal alarmed most of the parish clergy, who closed their pulpits against him. This drove him into the open air at Bristol (1739), where he founded the first Methodist Chapel, and then the Foundry at Moorfields, London, which became their headquarters. His life was frequently in danger, but he outlived all persecution, and the itineraries of his old age were triumphal processions throughout the country. He was a prolific writer, producing grammars, histories, biographies, collections of hymns, his own sermons and journals, and a magazine.*

*Adapted from http://www.biography.com/search/article.jsp?aid=9528077&search=John+Wesley (January 8, 2004).